# Fundamentals

## of

# Music

*by*

## RAYMOND ELLIOTT

*Associate Professor of Music*
*Texas Technological College*

Englewood Cliffs

•  PRENTICE-HALL, INC.  •

Library of Congress
Catalog Card Number:
55-5401

First printing.............January, 1955
Second printing..........September, 1955
Third printing.............. March, 1956
Fourth printing............ January, 1958
Fifth printing..............January, 1959
Sixth printing............. January, 1960

34128

*To a quartet of little women*
*whose love and devotion*
*made this book possible*
Annie Earl, mother
Helen Gould, wife
Roberta Annette, daughter
Phyllis Rae, daughter

# Preface

This book is designed to integrate theory, music-reading, and melodic ear-training. Its aim is to lay the foundations of musicianship through emphasis upon hearing and seeing rhythm and melody with a suggestion of their harmonic background. For the simplest and most effective presentation, a fundamental pattern is followed in each chapter.

The first part of each chapter deals with the rudiments of music. The elementary theoretical aspects of music are introduced and applied as needed. Thus scales, keys, time signatures, melodic design, and chords are woven through each chapter, making them an integral part of the music itself.

Harmony is the next consideration in each chapter. Since most melodic skips are made between the members of a chord, each new tonal problem is approached through the triad. The chord, with its passing and neighboring tones, is first presented and then immediately applied in the Melodies for Singing and Dictation. One of the chief factors in the selection of the melodies for each chapter was consideration of the particular chords and the intervals between their components. This, of course, does not mean that no other chords are implied in the melody; it simply means that the important emphasis is placed on the intervals of the chords under consideration. The new chord introduced in each chapter, with those presented previously, is indicated with Roman numerals in a few of the melodies. These should be played as the melodies are sung. The purpose of this procedure is to impart an introductory feeling for the harmonic background of melody. For further aid in hearing melodic intervals and harmony, the chords should be sung in arpeggio form.

The next division in each chapter is concerned with rhythm. Although most people have a natural response to meter in general, they are frequently weak in perceiving and responding to rhythmic patterns as represented by notation in the musical score. One way to strengthen the response to rhythmic patterns is the use of isolated rhythm drills which are to be tapped and counted. The author believes that such isolation is unnecessary and that rhythms should invariably be presented in a tonal setting. But in order that a minimum of difficulty is experienced, only one new rhythmic problem is introduced in each chapter. Rhythm as well as harmony has thus been incorporated as an important consideration in the selection of melodies for each chapter.

As has already been implied, the Melodies for Singing and Dictation, the next chapter division, contain the tonal and rhythmic problems introduced in each chapter.

The final chapter division contains suggestions for further study followed by a work sheet.

The appendix contains very simple conventional chord progressions which may be used in connection with the material of each chapter. These, of course, are keyboard harmony exercises and may be used as part of the assignment as recommended in Suggestions for Further Study at the close of each chapter.

## A NOTE ON MUSIC-READING

Music is a language, and for its fullest appreciation and comprehension one must achieve mastery of its techniques. The ability to read and understand music depends upon both the ear and the eye. The hearing must precede the eye for it is impossible to sing tones we cannot hear. In this respect it is like learning our mother tongue: we learn to speak it, by imitating what is heard, before learning to read it. It is only later that we learn the signs and symbols which represent sounds and objects. This is precisely the procedure in learning to hear and see music. And, as in language, it implies more than a recognition of symbols, for comprehension is the important essential; and comprehension involves a study of the structure of either language or music.

The first approach to reading music, then, is through listening, for music is an aural art. The second is through the eye; as in reading we comprehend through recognition of printed symbols, so in music we comprehend meaning through recognition of individual musical notations.

The first attempts at reading music can hardly be called sight-singing. Many repetitions are necessary for both ear and eye for easy recognition of tonal and rhythmic patterns with their various positions on the staff. The beginner consequently must master these patterns for fluency. The developing process of these fundamental skills is not sight-singing as such, but simply ear and eye training. Skill in music-reading develops gradually as the student reads more and more widely in various styles of music.

Although a general resemblance between reading a language and reading music has been pointed out, the specific problems in reading music are actually different from those in book reading since the habits and skills necessary to meet the requirements of good reading are different. Let us consider briefly three of the major differences.

1. In reading music the student must develop a feeling for the key. This means that he must hear the tonal relationship existing between the several tones of the key. He must hear, first, individual tones, then must aurally comprehend several at a time, as a group: a succession of tones as in melody, a group simultaneously as in harmony. The ear must learn to respond to about as many melodic intervals as there are letters in the English alphabet. The main difference between the phonetic qualities of alphabetical sounds and melodic intervals is that musical sounds exist in pitch relationship at a definite pitch and alphabetical sounds do not. This particular complexity calls for special training not at all required in book reading.

2. The act of seeing in music-reading is also more involved than in language. In music, the span of vision is one of breadth as well as linear dimension. In book reading the vertical distance is restricted to the height of the letters. Furthermore, the eye moves along in a single horizontal line, though this is by groups or "eye spans" rather than a single progression. In contrast, in reading music, the eye moves not only horizontally but vertically as well, and at many angles. Thus the problem is more complex spatially, the area varying between one-fourth and one-third of an inch; in other words, the distance from the space

below the staff to the space above the staff.[1] Reading piano or orchestral scores is even more involved.

3. Music offers a fundamental difference in the matter of rhythm. For example, the student must retain tones for definite lengths of time, at the same time anticipating, with appropriate comprehension, the pitch and length of tones following. There are about as many different note lengths as there are letters in the alphabet, and their combinations further complicate matters. Add these problems to those presented by intervals, and it will be easy to understand why the student must be mentally alert in order to hear and see music.


## ACKNOWLEDGMENTS

Acknowledgment is due the following publishers for use of melodies as follows:

Silver Burdett Company, Volume I of *The Progressive Music Series:* "Little Sister's Lullaby," p. 206; "Happy Thoughts," p. 219; "Polly's Bonnet," p. 189; "The Postman," p. 190; "Honey Bee," p. 245; "The Skipping Rope," p. 204; "At the Dance," p. 126; "Street Music," p. 226; "In May Time," p. 291; "In Wooden Shoes," p. 214; "Thanksgiving Day," p. 284; "Valentine Song," p. 216; "The Little Seeds," p. 133; "The Mulberry Bush," p. 199; "The Flower's Friend," p. 223; "Night and Morning," p. 297; "The Wizard," p. 299; "The Oriole's Nest," p. 236; "A Cat-Land Law," p. 288. Volume II of *The Progressive Music Series:* "New Day," p. 141; "Solitude," p. 190; "The Homesick Lowlander," p. 162; "The Raindrops," p. 233; "Noel," p. 263; "The Rainbow Dress," p. 182; "The Old Shepherd," p. 200; "In the Sleigh," p. 197; "Guessing Song," p. 140; "Dance of the Leaves," p. 188. From Volume III of *The Progressive Music Series:* "The Old Apple Tree," p. 184; "Happy Autumn Days," p. 143; "Summer's Done," p. 140; "In Ocean Cave," p. 198; "The Frost," p. 139; "My Bonny Pipes," p. 142; "Well Met, Well Met," p. 152; "The Maypole," p. 138; "Come, Lassies and Lads," p. 159.

C. C. Birchard Company, *Senior Laurel Songs:* "Peace Be With

---

[1] Otto Ortman, "Span of Vision in Note Reading," *Music Educators National Conference,* 1937, p. 88.

All," p. 125, Lithuanian Melody, arrangement by Hunt; "Pastoral," p. 157, Peruvian Folk Tune, arrangement by Winthrop; "The Three Sons," p. 13, Somerset Folk Song, arrangement by Hunt; "Carem Carmela," p. 228, Mexican Folk Tune, arrangement by Spaulding. *The School Song Book:* "A Life on the Ocean Wave," p. 33, by Russell.

American Book Company, *Hollis Dann Song Series,* Book Two: "In Spring," by Busch, p. 88, and for checking the copyright status of many melodies found in their publications.

Permission for reprint of "Obstination" by H. de Fontenailles granted by Durand et Cie, Paris, France; Elkan-Vogel Co., Inc., Philadelphia 3, Pennsylvania, Agents.

Heugel et Cie for reprint of "Elegy" by Massenet.

For their help in preparing this book grateful acknowledgment is made to the following: Professor Howard A. Murphy, Teachers College, Columbia University; Dr. Walter E. Nallin, City College of New York; Dr. Everett A. Gillis, Helen Elliott, Mary Jeanne van Appledorn, Dr. Gene Hemmle, Texas Technological College; Earl L. Weidner, New Jersey State Teachers College; James F. Leisy, Prentice-Hall, Inc.; Dr. Rogers Whitmore, University of Missouri; Raymond Stuhl, Jeannette Cass Stough, University of Kansas; Mildred Cook McClintock and Dow Mooney.

RAYMOND ELLIOTT

# Table of Contents

# ANALYTIC TABLE OF CONTENTS

## ANALYTIC TABLE OF CONTENTS (CONTINUED)

# • 1 •

# Tone and Its Representation

Music is a medium of expressing thought and feeling through tone and time. It is an art, and all forms of art are means through which beauty is expressed. The medium employed for the expression determines the type of art. Where the painter uses lines and color as his medium, and the sculptor uses stone or metal, the musician uses *tone* and *time*. Through these media he transfers his thoughts, emotions, and moods to others. He organizes his feelings and expresses them through the three elements of music—*rhythm, melody,* and *harmony*—whose combination is called *form*.

**Tone.** *Tone* is the result of regular vibrations. Irregular vibrations produce noise. A musical tone has four characteristics: namely, *pitch, length, quality,* and *quantity*. The *pitch* is determined by the number of vibrations per second: the higher the tone, the greater the number of vibrations per second; the lower the tone, the fewer the number of vibrations. The *length* or *duration* of the tone has to do with the interval of time during which the vibrations continue. The *quality* or *timbre* is concerned with the character or kind of tone produced. That is, tonal quality is determined by the producing instrument and its resonating capacity. The *quantity* or *intensity* refers to the degree of strength, force, or volume of the tone.

It is quite evident that the musician has a wide range in his media of tone and time. If he writes for a single voice, his choice of tone is naturally limited to the range and quality of that particular voice. This

1

is also true of a single instrument, with the exception of one with a very wide range, such as the piano. But when he is writing for a group of voices or instruments he is practically unlimited. Considering the timbre and range of the various voices and instruments, and the many combinations of their qualities and tones at different pitches and lengths, it is almost impossible to imagine the complexity of the material which the composer has at his disposal.

The task confronting us, then, is to train the ear, the eye, and the mind to comprehend this tonal material. To do this—that is, to acquire the ability to respond accurately to the four characteristics of tone—requires time, patience, concentration, self-analysis, and constructive criticism. Only those who put forth the necessary effort to obtain this skill earn the right to the title of musician, for such expertness is the essence of *musicianship*. From the very beginning, the student must approach the art with a scientific attitude, and his advance should be marked by accuracy and precision.

**Notation.** *Notation* is the representation of music on paper. The system with which we are so familiar, as is true of any language, was hundreds of years in the making. At first, music was transmitted orally, to the ear only; but as the art grew more complex, a means of conveying it to the eye was necessary. The result was the development of a system of signs by which the composer could convey his musical ideas to others.

One of the first of these signs to be developed was the note. The following notes are employed in modern notation:

**EX. 1-1**

whole . . . . . . . . . . . . . . . . . . . . . . . . . . . . . . . . . . . . . . . . . . . . . . . . . . ○

half . . . . . . . . . . . . . . . . . . . . . . . . . ♩

quarter . . . . . . . . . . . . . . ♩

eighth . . . . . . . . . . . . ♪

sixteenth . . . . . . . ♬

thirty-second . . . ♬

These symbols, representing tone lengths, are sometimes called *relative note-lengths* because each succeeding note is a fractional part of the whole note, and the time value is reckoned accordingly. For example, if four equal counts are given to the whole note, then the half note will receive two counts of the same length, the quarter one count, the eighth one-half of a count, and so on.

The round part of the note is called the *head,* the line attached to the head, the *stem,* and the curved line attached to the stem, the *hook.* Eighth, sixteenth, or thirty-second notes are often represented in groups by a straight line or lines attached to the stems, thus: These lines are called *beams* or *ligatures.*

An increase in the time value of notes may be designated by *dots,* which are placed at the right of the note head and which increase the time value of the note by one-half. That is, the dot receives one-half as much time as the note, thus:

Sometimes two dots are used by a note. In this case the second dot is one-half the value of the first, thus:

The symbols which represent a silent passage of time in music are called *rests;* they correspond to the note time-values. Rests, like notes, may be dotted, the time value increasing in conformity with the rule mentioned above. The following rests are used in modern notation:

**EX. 1-2**

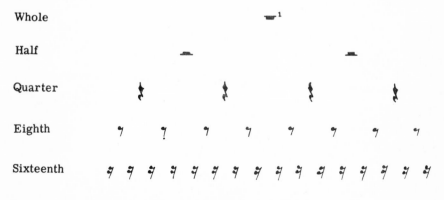

Whole [1]

Half

Quarter

Eighth

Sixteenth

Thirty-second

[1] The whole rest may be employed in a measure of any meter. See p. 145.

The five parallel lines on which notes and rests are placed are called the *staff*. Each line and each space of the staff is called a *degree*, of which there are nine—five lines and four spaces. The staff may be extended by adding short lines called *ledger-lines* above and below the regular lines. The degrees are numbered as follows:

EX. 1-3

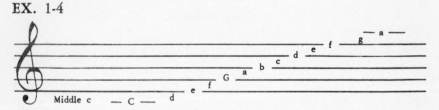

The degrees of the staff are named after the first seven letters of the alphabet. And since the staff would have little meaning if each degree did not represent a definite pitch, a sign called a *clef* is used. The two clefs in common use are the *G* (treble) and the *F* (bass).[2] They are so named because they were originally Gothic letters. Such a resemblance can be seen in our capital letters of the same name. When the *G* clef is placed on the second line of the staff (so said because it crosses it four times), it indicates that the second line of the staff is *G*. The names of the other degrees are calculated from *G*, as follows:

EX. 1-4

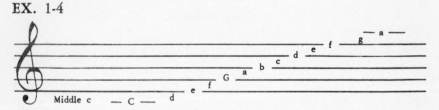

When the *F* clef is placed on the fourth line of the staff (so said because it originates there), it indicates that the fourth line of the staff is *F*. The names of the other degrees are calculated from *F*, in the following manner:

EX. 1-5

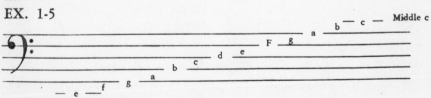

[2] The *C* clef on the third line, **B H B** locates Middle *C* on any line of the staff. When placed it is known as the alto clef; and when placed on the fourth line, the tenor clef. It is often used with orchestral instruments.

Actually, the G clef indicates that the second line of the staff is the first G above Middle C, and the F clef indicates that the fourth line of the staff is the first F below Middle C. Each is five degrees from Middle C.

These staves are often connected by a *brace,* which indicates that the music so joined is to be performed simultaneously, thus:

EX. 1-6

Now let us observe how these letters are applied to the piano. Its keyboard is composed of both black and white keys, the black keys being in alternate groups of twos and threes. C is always the first key to the left of two black keys. The one nearest the center of the keyboard is Middle C. To discover the relationship between the piano keyboard and the staves, find the second C below (to the left of) Middle C and play all the white keys upward (to the right), naming each key after the letter name of the staff degree. Continue to the C above Middle C, using the staves and keyboard on the following page.

This combination of the G and F clefs, as shown in Ex. 1-7, is known as the *great staff.* The duplication beginning on each eighth key of the piano and eighth letter of the staff is important. It is a repetition which occurs regularly throughout the entire keyboard. The difference in pitch from any letter name on the staff, or any key name on the piano, to the next corresponding letter or key, either up or down, is called an *octave,* for example: C, C; D, D; E, E; and so forth. Observe the names of the various octave groups, beginning on C. Any pitch within a given octave is named from the C immediately below it, thus: first space below bass clef is great F; fourth line, bass, small F; first space, treble, $F^1$, and so forth.

Now let us center our attention on the tones contained in the C-octave. Play the example on the top of page 7. This succession of tones is known as a *scale,* which may be in an ascending order as in (a), or a descending order as in (b). Most of our music is founded upon this series of tones. Still other tones, which we shall study later, are derived from this series.

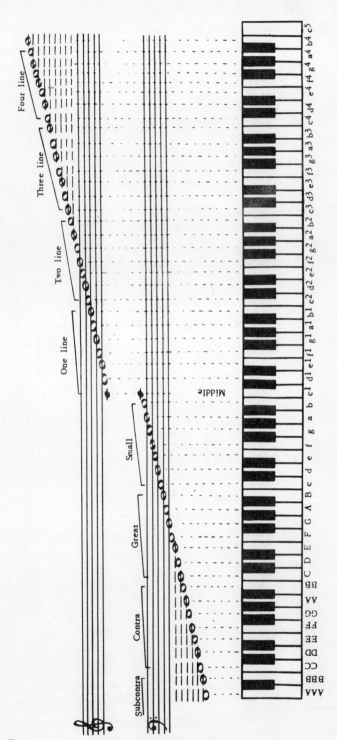

## EX. 1-8

These tones are definitely related to each other by natural laws of sound and must become so thoroughly familiar to us that we can hear any tone of the series from any given tone. This can be accomplished only by training ourselves to hear the allied tones and is the first important step in the training of the ear. It means that we must practice identifying each tone by its distinct character and by its special relationship to each of the others. It must be remembered that the ability to read music depends on the accuracy with which the ear can identify sounds. It is utterly impossible to sing tones we cannot hear. The ear, then, is the singer's guide. We learn to sing by imitating what we hear, much as we learn to speak a language; and since the series of tones given above is the foundation of the musical language, we must learn to imitate and recognize their sounds perfectly.

### SUGGESTIONS FOR FURTHER STUDY

Play and sing the scale many times in both *treble* and *bass,* using the following letters, syllables, and numerals.

$$c \quad d \quad e \quad f \quad g \quad a \quad b \quad c^3$$
do re mi fa sol la ti do
1 2 3 4 5 6 7 8

Pay particular attention to the relation of each tone to the other. *Listen carefully* to the quality and pitch of the tone produced by the piano and by your own voice, being sure to maintain a critical attitude. If you play any instrument other than the piano, play the scale on it for yourself and for the class, observing the quality of tone.

Play small divisions of the scale, such as *c, d, e; c, e; e, f, g; e, g;* etc. Sing each group immediately after playing. Now reverse the process: first sing small divisions of the scale, then test yourself at the piano. Be as critical of your work

[3] The letters are called *absolute pitch names* because each represents a definite pitch. The syllables and numerals are *relative pitch names,* because any pitch may be used for *do* (1), and because the other tones of the scale take their pitch in relation to the given pitch. The use of syllables is very old, having been employed by the Chinese, Hindus, and ancient Greeks. Our syllables are derived from the system invented by Guido of Arezzo (980–1050), who used the first syllable in each line of a Latin hymn to Saint John the Baptist—*ut, re, mi, fa, sol, la.*

as possible. Practice the exercises given above until you can hear the tones of the scale without singing them aloud.

Make a great staff by placing a dotted line representing Middle C between the treble and bass staffs. Name the lines and spaces on each staff, indicating their octave group.

Play c on the piano; think the pitch of c $^1$; sing it; play it.

Play c $^1$; think the pitch of c; sing it; play it.

Sound c $^1$ on the piano, and without further aid from the instrument sing other tones of the scale above or below. After each try, test with the piano. Practice this until you can sing any tone of the scale from c.

# • 2 •

# Meter and Measure

**Meter.** Sing the following well-known melody, observing the strong-weak pulsation:

EX. 2-1

Now sing the following familiar hymn, noting the strong-weak-weak pulsation:

EX. 2-2

These examples illustrate the basic accents which help to give vitality to music. The first moved in groups of twos (strong-weak), whereas the second was in groups of threes (strong-weak-weak). Such groups, with their schemes of accents, constitute *meter*. In the first example we felt a strong-weak pulsation known as *duple meter;* in the second a strong-weak-weak variety known as *triple meter.*

**Measure.** Each pulsation, whether strong or weak, is called a *beat*. The beats, with their regularly recurring accents, are always found in

9

groups of twos or threes, or a combination thereof, and are grouped into uniform *measures.* The *bar,* a perpendicular line drawn across the staff, indicates these groupings. The first beat following it is usually the strong part of the measure, but only in certain styles or periods. Sing the examples above again, observing that the strong accent occurs on the beat immediately following the measure bar.

Returning again to Ex. 2-1, we observe that there are two quarter notes or their equivalent in each measure, in conformance with the numerals $\frac{2}{4}$ found at the beginning of the example. The sign $\frac{2}{4}$ is known as the *metric* or *time signature;* the upper designating the number of beats to be found in each measure and the lower the kind of note which will receive a beat. Reading from the top downward, the signature denotes that there are two beats in each measure and that a beat is to be given to each quarter note. This, then, is in two-four time, or *duple* meter.

In Ex. 2-2 there are three quarter notes or their equivalent between each bar, as indicated by the metric signature. This example, then, is in three-four time, or *triple* meter.

To summarize, it must be remembered that the upper figure in any metric signature indicates the number of beats, pulses, or counts in a measure, and the lower, the kind of note receiving a beat. With this in mind, study the following:

EX. 2-3

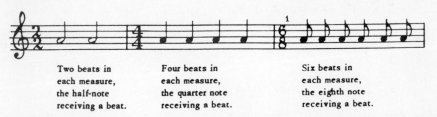

| Two beats in each measure, the half-note receiving a beat. | Four beats in each measure, the quarter note receiving a beat. | Six beats in each measure, the eighth note receiving a beat. |

The lower figure often varies according to the desire of the composer. Take the following for an example:

EX. 2-4

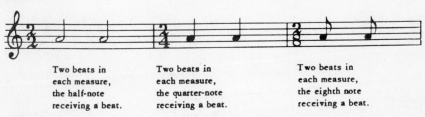

| Two beats in each measure, the half-note receiving a beat. | Two beats in each measure, the quarter-note receiving a beat. | Two beats in each measure, the eighth note receiving a beat. |

[1] See p. 68.

The selection of a unit or beat-note is purely a matter of choice and in no way affects the speed or character of the music. The illustrations in Ex. 2-4 are merely three different ways of indicating that there are to be two beats in each measure. We might print the word "cat" in a number of different types of letters, but the meaning of the word would remain unchanged. We may conclude, then, that a composition would sound the same whether it were written in $\frac{2}{2}$, $\frac{2}{4}$, or $\frac{2}{8}$.

To get a more vivid picture of these regularly recurring accents, let us compare them with the accents in poetry.

**EX. 2-5**

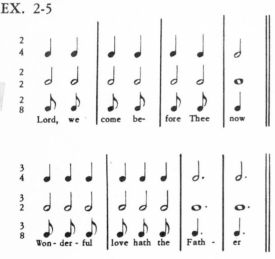

The first pulse in each group is accented and it occurs at regular time intervals, thereby producing measure.

The six meters in common use are illustrated below.

**EX. 2-6**

(a)  Duple Meter (Simple—one duple group in each measure)

(b)  Triple Meter (Simple—one triple group in each measure)

(c)  Quadruple Meter (Simple—one quadruple group in each measure)

(d) Compound Duple Meter—Sextuple
   (Two triple groups in each measure)

(e) Compound Triple Meter [2]       (f) Compound Quadruple Meter
    (Three triple groups in              (Four triple groups in
    each measure)                        each measure)

It is necessary for the musician to feel these groups of pulses because they are the foundation for more complex musical patterns. It should be noted, however, that all music does not begin on the accented part of the measure, as the following shows:

EX. 2-7

Praise | God from whom all | bless - ings flow ‖

**Conductor's pattern.** An excellent means of learning to feel such groups is to experience the physical manifestation of the conductor's beat. The two most important motions of his hand are (1) the *preliminary* or *preparatory beat* and (2) the *down beat*. The preliminary beat is a "get ready" movement of the hand which precedes the initial beat in the composition. It may be illustrated by the dotted line in the following representation of the conductor's beat pattern for duple and triple meter.

EX. 2-8

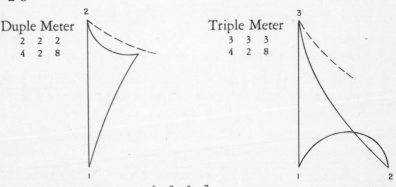

Duple Meter
2  2  2
4  2  8

Triple Meter
3  3  3
4  2  8

[2] Other time signatures such as $\frac{6}{16}$ $\frac{9}{16}$ $\frac{5}{4}$ $\frac{7}{4}$ are possible.

As may be seen, its direction is determined by the first beat in the composition. If the music begins on count one, the preparatory beat for duple meter originates as if on count two in the conductor's pattern and moves upward into position for the down beat, and for triple meter on count three. If the music begins on the fourth count in quadruple meter as in Ex. 2-7 above, the preparatory beat originates as if on count three and moves to the position for the count of four which begins the piece.[3] Whether the preliminary beat is quick or slow is determined by the nature of the piece it initiates. If the composition is a march, the "get ready" beat should be quick; if the music is somber, the preparatory beat should so indicate. The purpose of the preliminary beat is to prepare the performers. For singers and wind instrumentalists, it is the signal to breathe; for the violinists and other stringed instrumentalists, to get bow and fingers into position.

Many beginners encounter some difficulty in feeling the preliminary beat. Some have found it helpful to count aloud the beat on which the preliminary beat originates. Others use the words *sing* or *play* to initiate the preparatory beat.

The down beat is definite, confident, expectant. It should move straight down, hit an imaginary base, and bounce in the direction of the following beat. It is with the down beat that the conductor indicates the measure bar, and thus the strongest beat within the measure. It should be different and definite enough from other beats to ensure no doubt concerning it. The hand motions and counts for the duple and triple meters have already been given in Ex. 2-8, with the preliminary beat indicated by a dotted line. Use them as you sing Exs. 2-1 and 2-2 at the beginning of this chapter, and continue their use on the "Melodies for Singing" found later in this chapter.

**Meter, rhythm, and tempo.** Because of the confusion existing with reference to the terms meter, rhythm, and tempo, it might be of value at this point to define each briefly, more details being furnished in later chapters. *Meter* may be defined as the scheme of accents. *Rhythm* pertains to everything of a temporal or durational quality of tone, and therefore, in its broadest sense, to the tones and rests of different lengths within the meter. *Tempo* refers to the speed at which a composition is executed. In this regard, it must be emphasized that the metric signature in no way indicates the speed of the beats. The composer uses two pri-

---

[3] The upbeat, the last beat in a measure as in Ex. 2-7, is called *anacrusis*.

mary methods for indicating tempo, but since these will be discussed later, for the present the following terms expressive of tempo will serve our need:

Grave—slow and solemn

Lento—slow

Largo—large, broad, slow

Adagio—at ease, leisurely

Moderato—at moderate speed

Andante—going, moving at moderate rate

Allegro—cheerful, quick

Vivace—very lively

Presto—very, very lively

## MELODIES FOR SINGING AND DICTATION

The following melodies are in duple and triple meter and contain various note and rest lengths. Use the conductor's beat while the melodies are being played, and accent the down beat. Then sing them, using letters, syllables, and numbers. Keep a steady, even beat.

### MELODIES FOR SINGING

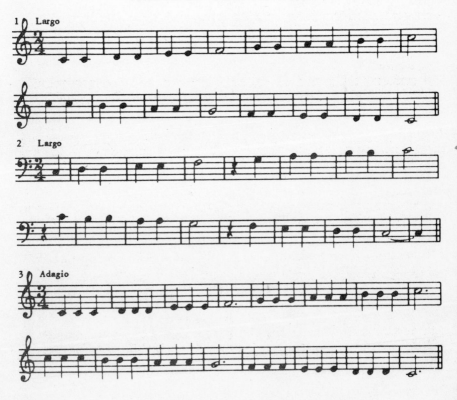

MELODIES FOR DICTATION

## SUGGESTIONS FOR FURTHER STUDY

Sound $c^1$ on the piano, and without further aid from the instrument, sing other tones of the scale above or below. Test with the piano.

[4] Since melodies 12 and 14 contain only one note in each measure, the teacher should use an accompaniment to aid the student in determining the meter.

Transcribe on the work sheet below several of the above Melodies for Dictation, substituting the *F* clef for the *G*, and the *G* clef for the *F*.

Write and play the *c* scale, ascending and descending, beginning on the following pitches: *C, c, c* [1].

Transcribe several of the above Melodies for Dictation, substituting

$$\frac{2}{4} \text{ for } \frac{2}{2}, \ \frac{2}{2} \text{ for } \frac{2}{4}, \ \frac{3}{4} \text{ for } \frac{3}{2}, \ \text{and } \frac{3}{2} \text{ for } \frac{3}{4}.$$

## *WORK SHEET*

# • 3 •

# Major Scales and Keys

## RUDIMENTS

Thus far we have played, sung, and written the scale from only one degree of the staff, namely C; but a scale may begin on any pitch or on any degree of the staff. This pitch, the tone on which it commences, furnishes the name of the scale and is called its *key tone*. For example, the C scale was so named because it began on C; C was its key tone. When we build a scale on any tone other than C, we follow a similar pattern. Since this is true, it is wise to learn more about the construction of this scale before attempting to form new ones.

**Scale formula.** To understand the formula of the C scale, we must become acquainted with some new musical terms. The first of these is the *interval*. An interval is the difference in pitch between any two tones. There are several of these in our musical language, but for the present we are concerned with only two, the *half step* and the *whole step*.[1] A clearer understanding of intervals may be obtained by reference to the piano keyboard (see keyboard below): from any key on the piano to the next key above or below, white or black, is a half step. Thus, going from C to the next key above (black), we go a half step. From this key to D we go another half step. The distance from C to D represents a whole step. We may conclude from this that the half step occurs when there is no key between, and the whole step occurs when there *is* a key between.

[1] Also called half or semitone and whole tone.

With this knowledge, we are now able to determine the successive intervals of the scale of C. Our examination of the piano keyboard reveals that there is a whole step between C and D; D and E; F and G; G and A; and A and B. Since there is no key between E and F, and B and C, the interval is that of a half step. The interval pattern of the scale is shown below:

EX. 3-1

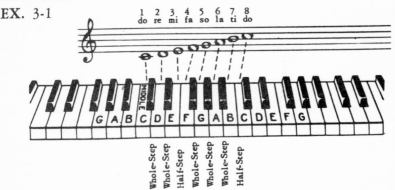

This is also the pattern or formula for all major scales and, since it is invariable, it should be committed to memory.

We have already learned that the tones of a scale are related to each other and to the key-tone. Consequently, let us think of the tones of a scale as representing a *family* of *related* tones called a *key*.[2] In the scale these occur in consecutive order, but when arranged in any other order, as in melody, and related to a central tone (the key tone), they are said to be the tones of a key. Sing the two examples on page 9 again, and notice that the tones are drawn to a central tone which is the center of gravity of the key.

The full name of a scale constructed according to the interval pattern given above is the *major diatonic scale*. It is what we mean when we commonly speak of a scale. The word *scale* comes from the Latin, *scala*, meaning a ladder. The word *major* refers to certain intervals that are larger than the corresponding intervals in the minor scale (which will be studied later). The word *diatonic* comes from the Greek: *dia*, through; and *tonos*, a tone or sound. The word literally means, through the tones of a scale or of a key. Actually, the tones belonging to any scale or key are diatonic tones; in this respect the major scale is typical.

**Tetrachords and the building of new scales.** Every scale is divisible into two equal parts called *tetrachords* (Greek: *tetra*, four; and

2 The term *key* as used here is not synonymous with the keys on the piano keyboard.

*chord,* a string or note), each of which contains the same intervals, namely, a half step between three and four of each group, and whole steps between the other tones. The two tetrachords are separated by the interval of a step, thus:

EX. 3-2

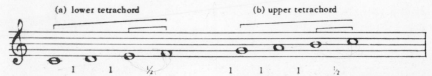

(a) lower tetrachord     (b) upper tetrachord

We are now ready to construct a new scale. Let us sing a scale from *G,* using the upper tetrachord of the scale of *C* as its basis, that is, as the lower tetrachord of the scale of *G.* Does it not sound the same as the scale on *C* except that all of the tones are higher? Now play the white keys on the piano from *G* to *G.* Do they sound the same as those you sang? The one necessary correction at the piano is the use of a black key for the seventh tone, in order to make the new scale sound as it should. In other words, the use of this black key makes the steps and half steps occur at the proper places. Compare the intervals of this new scale with those of the old.

In order to represent the new black key on the staff, it is necessary to place a character called a *sharp* (♯) before the note on *F.* When this symbol is placed on a degree of the staff, it causes that degree to represent a pitch one half step higher. Here is how the new scale appears on the staff and keyboard.

EX. 3-3

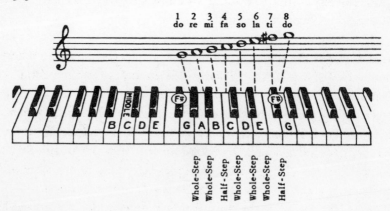

Since *F* sharp is a necessity of the new scale, it becomes an integral part of the key, and is therefore a *diatonic* tone, the new series of tones giving rise to a *new* scale and a *new* key (*G*). When music is written in this key, the sharp is placed on the fifth line of the treble staff and the fourth line of the bass staff, to the right of the clef. This is the sign of the key of *G*, and is known as the key signature. It indicates that each *F* on the staff is to be raised one half step to *F* sharp. Here is how the new scale appears in both the treble and bass staffs:

**EX. 3-4**

It should be noted again that, with the single exception of *F* sharp, the scale of *G* has the same tones as the scale of *C,* which suggests that the key of *G* is very closely related to the key of *C*.[4]

Now let us take the upper tetrachord of the scale of *G* for the lower tetrachord of another new scale, the scale of *D*. Sing the scale from *D*. Play it and notice that it is necessary to place a sharp on the seventh tone, *C,* of the new scale. The *F*, it should be noted, is also raised by a sharp, having been carried over in the tetrachord. In fact, all of the tones used were found in the *G* scale except *C* sharp. This suggests again that a close relationship exists between the two scales. The new scale as it appears on the staff and keyboard is shown below:

**EX. 3-5**

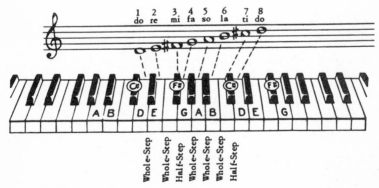

---

[3] Since *G* has become the key tone, the position of do, mi, sol, and do (1, 3, 5, and 8) should be observed very carefully.

[4] This relationship is explained more fully on pp. 107, 108.

The *F* sharp and the *C* sharp, being essential to the new key, are integral parts of it; in other words, diatonic tones. Therefore, they are placed on the staff following the clef in the order of occurrence and form the key signature of the key of *D* major (see p. 21).

EX. 3-6

The student should familiarize himself with these and other major sharp key signatures. These are shown on page 53. He should note the order of the sharps in the key signature carefully. The following rule may serve as a guide to the identification of the major keys using sharps: the last sharp in the key signature is *ti* (7); the next degree above is *do* (1). The name of the major key is always the same as the degree on which *do* (1) is found.

**Characteristics of scale tones.** If we study the tonal characteristics and individualities of the tones of the major scale, we find that some of them seem to be unsettled and to have a tendency to lead one to a more restful tone. We are not content to stop on re (2), fa (4), la (6), or ti (7), for any length of time. Re wants to lead us on to do or mi; fa to mi; la to sol; and ti to do. These four tones (re, fa, la, ti) are called *active tones,* and they resolve to the *rest tones* do, mi, and sol. This does not mean that ti must always resolve to do, fa to mi, or la to sol, for they do not always do so. It does mean, however, that unless they move along the scale in the opposite direction in such passages as mi, fa, sol; sol, la, ti, do; or do, ti, la, sol, the chances are they will resolve to their respective rest tones.

EX. 3-7            Resolution of Active Tones

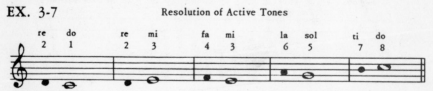

**The tonic chord.** And now, for the discovery of further aspects of tones of the scale, sing the first part of "The Marine's Hymn."

**EX. 3-8**

When sounded together, the first three tones of this well-known melody form the *tonic* chord, the term *tonic* being used in harmony to designate the first tone of the scale. Since there are three tones in this chord, it is known as a *triad,* which is a three-tone chord referred to as the *tonic* (or I) *triad.* Note that all members of the chord are on adjacent lines, or alternate degrees of the staff. Other chords which will be studied later are constructed in like manner. In each case, the members are on adjacent lines or spaces, depending on whether the lowest tone is located on a line or space. The lowest tone of the chord is called the *root.* Since the next member is three degrees up (*C D E*) from the root, it is called
                                                              1  2  3
the *third.* The highest tone is called the fifth because it is on the fifth degree above the root (*C D E F G*). Although the chord is identified
                          1  2  3  4  5
by the arrangement on alternate staff degrees of root, third, and fifth, the chord tones may be arranged in any order, as shown below:

**EX. 3-9**

These arrangements do not change the name of the chord since it remains a combination of *C, E,* and *G,* but the individual members of the chord may be in different positions. In Ex. 3-9 above, (a) is called the position of the fifth, since the fifth is highest; (b) the position of the

―――――――
[5] See Chapter 10 for explanation of *mf* and other marks of expression.

root, since the root is highest; and (c) the position of the third, since the third is highest.

A further observation is that the root, third, or fifth of the chord may occur as the lowest tone of the chord. The Roman numeral standing alone, as at *a* above, indicates that the lowest tone of the chord is the root. This is known as the fundamental position. The figure six used in connection with the Roman numeral, as at *b,* indicates that the root of the chord is found six staff degrees above the lowest tone of the chord.[6] When this is true, the third (*E*) is the lowest tone of the chord. This last arrangement of tones is known as the first inversion of a triad (inversions will be discussed later). The use of the six and four with the Roman numeral, as at (*C*), indicates that the third (*E*) and the root (*C*) are respectively six and four staff degrees above the lowest tone of the chord. This arrangement leaves the fifth (*G*) as the lowest tone of the chord, and is known as the second inversion of a triad.

In like manner, a triad may be built upon each tone of the scale. Examples of these will be introduced as needed in subsequent chapters. The student should keep in mind two objectives in the study of each chord: (1) the ability to hear, sing, and write the members of a chord; (2) the ability to hear the total effect of a chord as it is played, especially during the singing of some of the melodies.

The tonic (I) chord is the central chord of our tonal system, and nearly all compositions begin and end on some member of it.

**Passing and neighboring tones.** When a melody moves along the scale line from one member of a chord to another, the intervening tones are known as *passing tones.* However, if the melody progresses from a member of a chord to an adjoining degree (above or below) and returns to the original position, the middle tone is called a *neighboring tone* or a *turning tone.* The passing and neighboring tones of the tonic chord are represented below by black-faced notes.

**EX. 3-10**

(a) Passing tones of the Tonic Chord in *C*

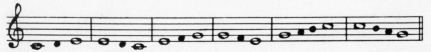

---

[6] In counting staff degrees, the student should be cautioned that the numbering is inclusive; that is, it begins with *E* and ends with *C*: E F G A B C
　　　　　　　　　　　　　　　　　　　　　　　　　1 2 3 4 5 6

(b)   Neighboring Tones of the Tonic Chord in *C*

**The phrase.** A single tone or chord, regardless of its beauty, has far less significance than a succession of related tones or chords; these produce values in thought and feeling inexpressible by a single tone or single chord. In music that we call beautiful, such successions are organized logically and effectively. Two of these are the *motive* and the *phrase.* The motive is the smallest of music ideas and is the germinal thought of a composition. This small melodic fragment of a musical theme or subject is often distinguishable by slight interruptions analogous to commas in a sentence within the phrase. The motive is often repeated exactly or in modification in developing logical coherence. A phrase may be defined as a musical idea possessing a certain degree of completion. It is usually, though not always, four measures in length. All music should be thought of in terms of these groups. Motives and phrases may be observed in The Melodies for Singing.

**Aids to reading music.** By this time, the student undoubtedly has made a few observations which will aid him in reading music at sight. They may be summed up as follows:

1.  If do (1) is on a line, mi (3), sol (5), and ti (7) are on the lines above.

2.  If do (1) is in a space, mi (3), sol (5), and ti (7) are in the spaces above.

3.  If do (1) is on a line, its octave above and below are in spaces.

4.  If do (1) is in a space, its octave above and below are on lines.

5.  In other words, do (1), mi (3), sol (5), and ti (7) are always similarly placed either on lines or in spaces, whereas octaves are dissimilarly placed.

## RHYTHM

**Quadruple meter and the divided beat.** Some of the Melodies for Singing which follow are in quadruple meter (see p. 11). The conductor's beat pattern is as indicated in Ex. 3-11.

Other melodies contain examples of the divided beat. To understand and gain a feeling for this new rhythmic problem, sing the first phrase of "Yankee Doodle." (Ex. 3-12.)

EX. 3-11

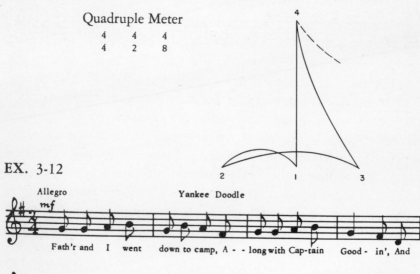

Quadruple Meter

| 4 | 4 | 4 |
|---|---|---|
| 4 | 2 | 8 |

EX. 3-12

Allegro — *mf* — Yankee Doodle

Fath'r and I went down to camp, A - - long with Cap-tain Good - in', And

Unknown

there we saw the men and boys As thick as has- ty pud - din'.

The metric signature indicates that there are two beats in each measure
and that the quarter note will receive a beat; yet it is evident that there
are twice as many notes in each of the first three measures as there are
beats. This is due to the fact that the beat note (the quarter note) has
been divided into two equal parts, which results in two notes for each
beat. Use the conductor's beat as you sing "Yankee Doodle" again, observing this equal division of the beat note.

## MELODIES FOR SINGING AND DICTATION

The melodies in this chapter contain skips between the members
of the tonic chord as well as the passing and neighboring tones. At times,
other harmonies than the tonic may be implied, but our major attention
must center upon the skips between the members of the tonic chord.
This chord, when indicated (by the Roman numeral I under the staff),
should be played by the teacher or a member of the class as the melodies
are sung. Concentrate upon hearing the skips between members of the
chord, and the total aural effect when the tones are sounded simultaneously. Occasionally the student may notice a note in the melody which
does not belong to the chord. Such a note may be a passing or neighboring tone.

# MELODIES FOR SINGING

7 See p. 145 for explanation for repeat dots.

⁸ See p. 3 for explanation of beams.

## MELODIES FOR DICTATION

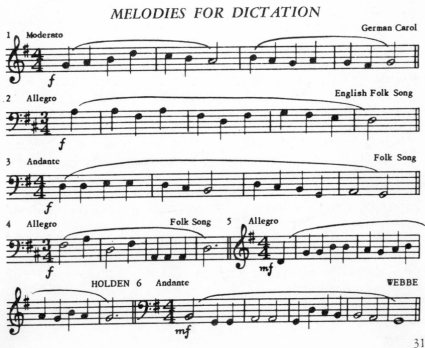

## SUGGESTIONS FOR FURTHER STUDY

Sing the Melodies for Singing again in the following manner: with one continuous sweep of the eye try to perceive an entire phrase. Close your eyes; visualize it; sing it mentally; then sing it aloud.

Write the Melodies for Dictation in quadruple meter in $\frac{4}{2}$ and $\frac{4}{8}$

Identify the passing and neighboring tones of the tonic chord in the Melodies for Singing and Dictation. Find examples of these passing tones in music familiar to you.

Add the upper tetrachord to the lower tetrachords in Sec. *a* of the work sheet which follows, and write in the necessary sharps. Use the piano keyboard in working out the whole and half steps. After writing the scale, place the sharps in the key signature to the right of the additional clef provided and indicate the position of do (1), mi (3), and sol (5). For proper placement of the sharps in the key signature, see p. 53. Play and sing each scale slowly. Play do (1), mi (3), and sol (5) slowly in successive order and then simultaneously, listening to the total effect.

[9] See p. 53 for explanation of this key signature.

Write, play, and sing the following melody in the keys of *G, D, A,* and *E* on the work sheet at (b):

Play the tonic chord, Appendix A, No. 1, in keys employing sharps in their signature.

## WORK SHEET
### (a)

(b)

# • 4 •

# Major Scales and Keys

## (Continued)

**Other major scales.** Sing the scale ascending from *F*. Play the white keys on the piano from *F* to *F*. Do they sound the same as those you sang? The one necessary correction at the piano is the use of a black key for the fourth tone, in order to make the new scale sound as it should and the half-step occur at the proper place. Compare the intervals of this scale with those of the scale formula presented in Chapter 3.

In order to represent the new black key on the staff it is necessary to place a character called a *flat* (♭) on *B*. When this symbol is placed on a degree of the staff, it causes that degree to represent a pitch one half step lower. The new scale appears on the staff and the keyboard in Ex. 4-1.

Since the *B* flat is essential to the new scale, it becomes an integral part of the key of *F* and is, therefore, a diatonic tone. When music is written in this key, the flat is placed on the third line of the treble staff and on the second line of the bass staff, to the right of the clef. This is the sign of the key of *F;* and as the key signature, it indicates that each *B* on the staff is to be lowered one half step to *B* flat. The scale appears on both the treble and bass staffs in Ex. 4-2.

36

## EX. 4-1

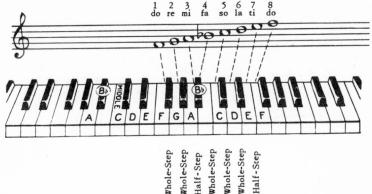

## EX. 4-2

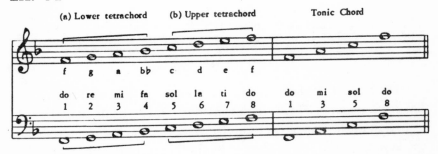

The student may have observed that the procedure in building this scale is a reversal of that used in the preceding chapter. Instead of counting *up* five degrees to find the key tone as was done in Chapter 3, we now count *down* five degrees to find the key tone of the new scale. It may also be observed that the lower tetrachord of the scale of *C* becomes the upper tetrachord of the scale of *F*, a phenomenon the opposite of that for the scales where sharps were employed. It may be noted further that the key of *F* has the very same tones as the key of *C*, with the exception of *B* flat: one reason why the key of *F* is said to be related to the key of *C*.

Now let us take the lower tetrachord of the scale of *F* for the upper tetrachord of another new scale, the scale of *B* flat. Again we find it necessary to place a flat on the fourth degree of the new scale. The staff and keyboard representation of this new scale is shown in Ex. 4-3 on the following page.

The flats (*B* flat and *E* flat) are now placed on the third line and the fourth space of the staff (second line and third space in the bass) to form the key signature of the key of *B* flat major. (See Ex. 4-4.)

## EX. 4-3

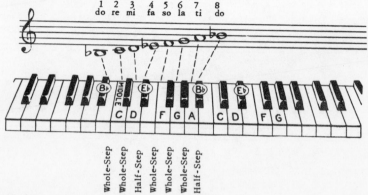

## EX. 4-4

(a) Lower tetrachord  (b) Upper tetrachord   Tonic Chord

do  re  mi  fa  sol  la  ti  do   do  mi  sol  do

The student should familiarize himself with these and other major flat key signatures. These are shown on p. 53. He should note the order of flats in the key signature carefully. As a guide to the identification of the keys employing flats, observe the following fact: since the last flat in the key signature is fa (4), count down four degrees to find do (1). If there is more than one flat in the key signature, do (1) will be on the same degree as the flat preceding the last one in the signature.[1]

## HARMONY

**The Dominant Chord.** As an introduction to the tones of the new chord we shall now consider, sing the following well-known melody:

### EX. 4-5

[1] See p. 53.

In the sixth measure (bracketed) we discover a tonal pattern new to us, the tones of the *dominant* chord. The dominant chord is built on the fifth tone of the scale, which in the key of *G* is *D*. Spelling this chord from the root with alternate letters or adjacent spaces, we find its members to be *D, F♯* and *A*. In example 4-5 the melody skips from the root up to the fifth and down to the third. The dominant chord is so named because the fifth tone of the scale and the chord built upon it have a dominating influence. This chord, which in importance is second only to the tonic, is identified by the Roman V. It is shown below as it appears in the key of *C*:

**EX. 4-6**

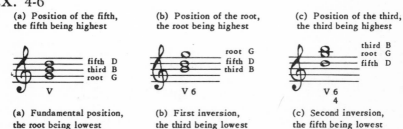

| (a) Position of the fifth, the fifth being highest | (b) Position of the root, the root being highest | (c) Position of the third, the third being highest |
|---|---|---|
| fifth D / third B / root G | root G / fifth D / third B | third B / root G / fifth D |
| V | V 6 | V 6 4 |
| (a) Fundamental position, the root being lowest | (b) First inversion, the third being lowest | (c) Second inversion, the fifth being lowest |

The dominant chord is also important for the part it plays in the formation of phrases. We learned in Chapter 3 that a phrase is usually four measures in length and that it possesses a certain degree of completion.[2] It can now be added that each phrase ends with a cadence, a term meaning a close or fall which conveys the impression of a temporary or permanent conclusion. The type of cadence is determined by the choice of chord or chords coming at its close. When the phrase ends on the dominant chord, the cadence is known as the *half cadence* or close. When it ends on the tonic chord, preceded by the dominant triad, the close is known as an *authentic cadence.* The student must become increasingly conscious of phrases and the chord or chords which mark their endings. The Melodies for Singing found in this chapter contain examples of the half and authentic cadence.

Passing and neighboring tones in relation to the members of the dominant chord are shown in Ex. 4-7.

## RHYTHM

**The tie and dot.** For a new experience in rhythm, sing the melody in Ex. 4-8.

[2] Phrases vary in length. The four measure phrase is found more frequently. However, the first phrase of "Come Thou Almighty King" (Ex. 2-2) is three measures long while the first phrase of "America" (Ex. 4-9) is six measures in length.

EX. 4-7

It may be noted in this selection that the first note in the second and fourth measures is held for a beat and one-half, and that the second eighth note is sung as the last half of count two. Furthermore, the first eighth note in each case is not articulated, the pitch of the quarter note being prolonged through the durational value of both the quarter and the eighth. The symbol indicating this prolongation is a curved line called the *tie*. The tie welds two or more successive notes of the same pitch into a single sound equal to the combined durations of the notes so tied. As may be observed, only the first of the connected or tied notes is articulated, the second continuing automatically through the total time value of all notes concerned. The tie is particularly useful in combining into a single duration two notes which are separated by the measure bar.

Another way of indicating extended duration of tones is by the dot, which may be illustrated by a repetition of the same passage. (See Ex. 4-9.)

Here the *dot* in measures two and four has replaced the tie. As explained in Chapter 1, p. 3, a dot to the right of a note increases the time value of the note by one-half. Thus the time value of the dotted quarter in Ex. 4-9 is that of a quarter plus an eighth note. This, of course, consists of the same time value represented by the tie in Ex. 4-8, as may be seen by comparing the two. A further example of the use of the dot may be found in the last note of the passage. Here the value of the dot is that

of a quarter, or one-half the value of the half note. Thus, the time value of the dotted half note here is that of three quarter notes. These could also be indicated by the tie in either of the following manners:

## MELODIES FOR SINGING AND DICTATION

The melodies which follow contain examples of the skips between members of the tonic and dominant chords and of the dot. The I and V chords should be played on the piano as indicated in the melodies.

### MELODIES FOR SINGING

[3] See page 142 for information concerning the fermata.

42

Night Song, Opus 23 No. 4 SCHUMANN

Chorus of Shepherds SCHUBERT

Come Unto These Yellow Sands, MARTINI

Love Songs, Waltz No. 9 BRAHMS

From Symphony No. 9 BEETHOVEN

German Melody, Arr. BRAHMS

19 Moderato

*mf*

Impromptus, op. 142 No. 2    SCHUBERT

20 Andante

*mp* I    I    I    14 V    I

I    V6    I    V    I    I    V

French Folk Song

I    I6    I    V    I

## MELODIES FOR DICTATION

1 Allegro    Arr. BRAHMS

*f*

2 Allegro    French Folk Song

*f*

3 Moderato    French Folk Song

*mf*

45

17 Adagio

Sanctus, Mass in G MOZART

18 Moderato

Impromptu, Op. 142 No. 2 SCHUBERT

English Folk Song

19 Allegro

20 Adagio

Sonatina, Op. 36 No. 3 CLEMENTI

Seraphic Song RUBENSTEIN

21 Andante

Sunday Morning, Op. 77 No. 1 MENDELSSOHN

22 Moderato

23 Moderato

MORLEY

## SUGGESTIONS FOR FURTHER STUDY

Sing the Melodies for Singing again in the following manner: with one continuous sweep of the eye try to perceive an entire phrase. Close your eyes; visualize it; sing it mentally; then sing it aloud.

Examine several of your favorite compositions for examples of the dot.

Add the upper tetrachord to the lower tetrachord in Sec. *a* of the work sheet which follows, and write in the necessary flats. Use the piano keyboard in working out the whole and half steps. After writing the scale, place the flats in the key signature to the right of the clef provided and indicate the position of do (1), mi (3), and sol (5). For proper placement of the flats in the key signature, see p. 53. Play and sing each scale slowly. Play do (1), mi (3), and sol (5) slowly in successive order, and then simultaneously, listening to the total effect.

Write the dominant chord in the position of the fifth in the keys given in Sec. *b* of the work sheet.

Examine the Melodies for Singing above and other folk songs with which you are familiar for examples of motives, and for half and authentic cadences.

Play the tonic and dominant chord progressions, Appendix A, No. 2, in all keys.

## WORK SHEET
### (a)

(b)

# • 5 •

# Review of Major Scales

## RUDIMENTS

**The circle of fifths.** If the student has followed the tetrachordal system in writing the major scales as presented and assigned for writing in Chapters 3 and 4, he has discovered fifteen key tones from which scales may be built. It will be recalled that the upper tetrachord became the lower tetrachord of each succeeding scale requiring an additional sharp. Using this pattern, we discovered the following key tones, each of which was found to be five staff degrees up from the preceding one. These key tones were assigned as part of the Work Sheet in Chapter 3, as follows: *C, G, D, A, E, B, F♯,* and *C♯*. The use of *F♯* and *C♯*

(instead of *F* and *C*) as key tones may seem surprising. Yet if we re-examine the upper tetrachords of the scales assigned for writing in Chapter 3, it will be noted that *F♯* and *C♯* were the beginning tones of the upper tetrachords of the *B* and *F♯* scales respectively. Further proof exists of the necessity for these sharped degrees in the fact that an equal number of half steps (7) exists between any key tone and the one immediately following, that is, *C* to *G, G* to *D,* and so on. In addition, we have already learned from our study of chords that the interval from *C* to *G* is a fifth, embracing as it does five degrees of the staff. Five staff degrees are also involved in the intervals of *G* to *D, D* to *A, A* to *E, E* to *B, B* to *F♯* , and *F♯* to *C♯* as well as seven half steps. These fifths, as will be learned in Chapter 11, are *perfect fifths.*

Turning now to review the scales employing flats, we will recall that the lower tetrachord of a scale became the upper tetrachord in a succession of scales having an additional flat. Consequently, the following key tones, each of which was five staff degrees down from the preceding one, were presented in the Work Sheet of Chapter 4:   C, F, B♭, E♭, A♭, D♭, G♭, and C♭.   The necessity of having these flatted degrees as key tones is that each succeeding key tone is a perfect fifth below the preceding one.

The series of fifteen key tones (C being common) just discussed may be arranged in a circle showing the succession of fifths from one key tone to the next, a figure which is known as the *circle of fifths*, which is shown on page 53 with the key signatures in treble and bass.

The student must keep in mind the relationship existing between a given scale and its *attendant scales*. By attendant scales we mean those that immediately precede and follow a given scale. This is more easily understood when we recall that the upper tetrachord of a given scale, C scale in Ex. 5-1 is the lower tetrachord of another scale, G, and that the lower tetrachord of C, the given scale, is the upper tetrachord of F.

**EX. 5-1**

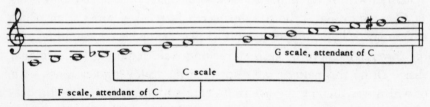

**Repetition and contrast.** In singing the melodies in previous chapters, the student may have already observed certain repetitions of motives and phrases. Repeated at the same pitch, such musical ideas are known as *exact repetition*; re-stated at a higher or lower pitch, they are known as a *sequence*. In some cases, there were slight tonal and rhythmic variations. As the essence of repetition, these uses are of great importance in giving unity to a melody. As a re-examination of the melodies already studied will reveal, such repetition is extensively used. For example, observe the use of repetition in Melody No. 1, p. 29.

In singing previous melodies, the student may also have observed new melodic ideas which, because of their rhythm and intervals, did not violate the basic unity of the melody. This skillful use of new but related materials illustrates the principle of contrast and serves the purpose of giving variety to music. For examples of the use of contrast,

EX. 5-2

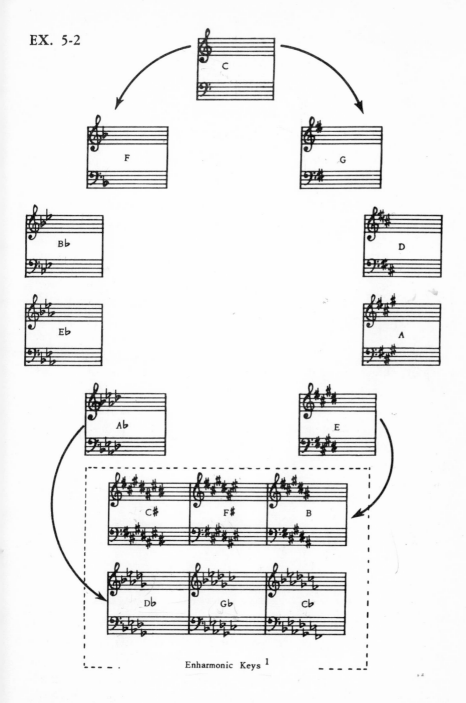

Enharmonic Keys [1]

the student should examine the following: No. 17, p. 44, and No. 7, p. 58.

[1] Enharmonic tones have the same pitch but different letter names.

To summarize what has just been said, it may be stated that unity is achieved through repetition, and variety through contrast. It is through the combined use of these principles that the composer develops continuity and balance.

## HARMONY

The subdominant chord. Sing the following familiar melody:

EX. 5-3

An unfamiliar tonal pattern appears in the second measure of this melody (bracketed), the skips between the chord tones of the *subdominant* or *underdominant* chord (IV). As may be observed, the chord originates on the fourth tone of the scale, and the other members are found in adjacent spaces. Its three positions, as it occurs in the key of *C*, are as follows:

EX. 5-4

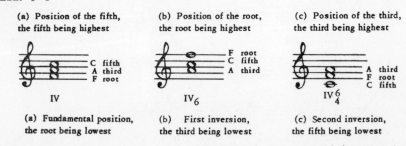

It is sometimes held that the subdominant is so-named because it is under the dominant in the ascending scale. Actually, as shown in Ex. 5-5, it is so-called because the subdominant (IV) is found a fifth below the tonic (I), whereas the dominant (V) is found a fifth above the tonic. In other words, IV is an underdominant of the tonic. Hence the prefix *sub* or *under*.

These three chords are known as the *principal triads* of the major key, and, as shown in the second part of the example below, these

54

EX. 5-5

IV  I  V

combined tones are those found in the major diatonic scale. The passing
and neighboring tones of the subdominant chord are shown below.

EX. 5-6

(a)                          Passing Tones

Neighboring Tones

## RHYTHM

**The tie and the slur.** The tie was defined and explained in the
preceding chapter in connection with the dot. Further examples of it
follow in the Melodies for Singing. These should be noted carefully
as the melodies are sung. The same symbol, a curved line, used for
the tie is also used for the slur.[2] In its capacity as a slur, the line is used
to connect consecutive notes representing different pitches. In its use
in instrumental music (to be considered more fully in a later chapter),
it means that the notes concerned are to be performed smoothly. In
vocal music, it indicates that the tones so joined are to be sung to one
word or syllable.

## MELODIES FOR SINGING AND DICTATION

The following melodies contain examples of the chord tones of the
subdominant chord, as well as of the dot, tie, and slur:

### MELODIES FOR SINGING

1   Andante

*mf*

[2] Although the slur is not a rhythmic device, it is introduced here in connection with
the tie since the same symbol is used for both.

Prayer of Thanksgiving    Dutch

2    Moderato

*mf*

Air de Ballet, Alceste    GLUCK

3    Allegro

*mf*

Duke Street    HATTON

56

Somerset Folk Song

From The Magic Flute   MOZART

There's Music In The Air   ROOT

57

12 Andante

mp   I   I   V   I   V   I   IV

I   I   I₆   V   I   V

Austrian Folk Song

IV   I   I₆   IV   I₆   V   I

American Indian Melody

13 Andante

mp

14 Allegro mp

We're called _____ Gon-do-lier-i, but that's a va-

ga-ry, it's quite hon-or-a-ry the trade that we ply _____

We're Called Gondolieri from The Gondoliers   SULLIVAN

15 Moderato p

How   love-ly   is   thy   dwell-ing   place,   o

Lord _____ of   hosts,   o   Lord   of   hosts

16 Allegro mf

The   first   No-el   the   an-gels did   say Was to cer-tain poor
They   look-ed   up   and   saw   a   star Shin-ing in   the

shep-herds in   fields as they   lay;   In   fields   where they   lay   keep-ing their
East   be-yond   them   far,   And   to   the   earth   it   gave   great

59

sheep On a cold win-ter's night that was so deep. No - el, No-
light And so it con - tin-ued both day and night.

The First Noel. Traditional

el, No - el, No - el, Born is the King of Is - ra - el

**17** Andante
*mf*

3) My Sun DI CAPUA

**18** Allegro

Christ the Lord is ris'n to - day Al - - - le - - lu - - ia
I    V6  I   IV6 IV  I                        I6/4  V  I

Christ The Lord Is Ris'n Today. From DAVIDICA

Sons of men and an - gels say: Al - - - le - - lu - - ia
IV6 I  IV  I6                  I6/4  V        I6/4  V  I

## MELODIES FOR DICTATION

**1** Allegro                              Somerset Folk Song
*f*

**2** Allegro                              English Folk Song
*mf*

³ See p. 122 for explanation of the triplet.

## SUGGESTIONS FOR FURTHER STUDY

Write from memory the key signatures in bass and treble at (a) on the work sheet.

Identify the key signatures of several of your favorite compositions. Also look for examples of the dot, tie, and slur.

Write the I, IV, and V chords, position of the fifth, in the keys of *C, G, D, A, F, B♭, E♭, A♭* on the work sheet at (b). Play them for total effect.

Note the phrases ending on the tonic and dominant chords and the use of the V to I progression in the final cadence of the above Melodies for Singing.

Examine the melodies in this and preceding chapters for examples of repetition and contrast.

Play the tonic and subdominant chord progressions, Appendix A, No. 3, in all keys.

# WORK SHEET

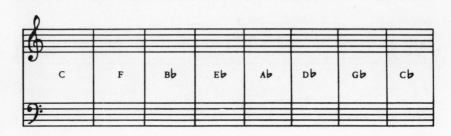

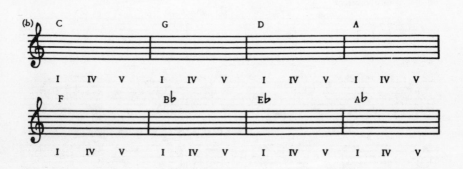

# · 6 ·

# Tempo

## RUDIMENTS

**Tempo indications.** Tempo is an Italian word used to express the speed at which a composition is executed. Many of the terms used in the interpretation and expression of music come from the Italians, who were the first to make wide use of such designations. Prior to 1600, tempo marks were almost unknown, since the rate of speed was expressed by the notation itself; that is, the beat and note values had absolute duration, only slight variations in speed being possible. But with the introduction of special words to denote tempo, a wide variety of speeds were made possible. Terms from other languages may also be found in music, since many composers prefer the use of their native tongues. In addition to words, or in conjunction with them, the composer may also use readings from an instrument called the *metronome* to indicate different rates of speed.

The metronome, by means of an inverted, swinging pendulum, the speed of which is controlled by a sliding weight, produces a set number of clicks per minute. If the pendulum weight, for example, is set at 60, the metronome will give sixty clicks per minute, each click representing a beat. In designating metronome speed, the composer uses a formula: M.M. ♩ = 60, or M.M. ♪ = 60, or M.M. ♪ = 60. The letters M.M. signify Maelzel's metronome—named after Maelzel, its inventor. In slow tempos of compound meter such as $\frac{6}{8}$ $\frac{9}{8}$ $\frac{12}{8}$ the composer uses the eighth note in his metronomic markings, and in fast tempos the dotted quarter: for example, M.M. $\eighthnote = 72$, M.M. $\dottedquarter = 72$. By the use of metronomic formulas, the composer is able to indicate precisely the rate of speed at which he wishes his composition to move.

The more recent electric metronomes are superior to Maelzel's for the reason that they are absolutely accurate and easier to manipulate. No winding or setting of a sliding weight is necessary; the instrument is simply plugged into an electric outlet and the dial set at the speed desired. Moreover, the speed may be changed without stopping the instrument by merely turning the dial. Some of the electrical metronomes use a click to indicate the beat, others a flash of light.

Before the invention of the metronome, the composer could not provide a definite indication of tempo; he could only use words to express in a general way what his wishes were in regard to speed. The most common of these terms, already given in chapter 2, may be repeated for review.

| | |
|---|---|
| **Grave**—slow and solemn | **Andante**—going, moving at moderate rate |
| **Lento**—slow | |
| **Largo**—large, broad, slow | **Allegro**—cheerful, quick |
| **Adagio**—at ease, leisurely | **Vivace**—very lively |
| **Moderato**—in moderate tempo | **Presto**—very, very lively |

Most of the words given above may be modified by the endings *etto* and *ino,* which diminish, or *issimo,* which increases the effect of the word so modified. Thus *allegretto* indicates a tempo somewhat slower than allegro, and *allegrissimo* a more rapid speed than allegro. Sometimes phrases which have historically identified traditional musical forms, such as *tempo di minuette* (in the time of the minuet), are used to indicate tempo. The words listed above are also combined sometimes with one another, and with other words. Although to list and define these combinations is not the object of this textbook, certain of them should become familiar to the student. Study the following miscellaneous words and phrases:

| | |
|---|---|
| **A**—at, for, with | **Assai**—very |
| **Animato**—animated | **Ben**—well |
| **A poco a poco**—little by little | **Ben marcato**—well marked |

| | |
|---|---|
| Cantabile—in a singing style | Piu—more |
| Con—with | Poco—a little |
| Con moto—with motion | Quasi—almost |
| Con spirito—with spirit | Risoluto—in a resolute manner |
| Farza—force or emphasis | Rubato—robbed |
| Grandioso—grandly | Simplice—simply |
| Grazioso—gracefully | Sempre—always |
| Ma—but | Simile—in the same manner |
| Marcato—marked | Sostenuto—sustained |
| Meno—less | Sotto voce—in a subdued manner |
| Mezzo—half | Tranquillo—tranquilly |
| Molto—much | Troppo—too, too much |
| Non—not | Vigoroso—vigorously |

If the composer wishes the tempo to be increased or decreased during the rendition of a composition in order to give variety and to make it more intelligible, he indicates these changes by such expressions as *ritardando* and *accelerando*. The most common of these terms, with the abbreviations by which they are sometimes indicated, are as follows:

Accelerando (accel.)—accelerating
Poco a poco animato—animated little by little
Ritardando (rit.)
Rallentando (rall.) ⎫—gradually retarding
A tempo—in the original tempo
Ad libitum (ad lib.)—at the performer's pleasure

As was intimated above, this list is incomplete, but it is sufficient to give the student a working knowledge of the terms used to indicate tempo. It is well to state here that some of the modern composers use English words to express their desires with regard to tempo and expression.

**Perfect and imperfect authentic cadence.** In Chapter 4 we learned that the dominant to tonic progression at the close of a phrase was known as the authentic cadence, so called because these chords establish the key. Such a close is said to be *perfect* when the melody ends on the key tone and *imperfect* when the melody ends on the third or fifth of the tonic chord. For example, a V-I progression (fundamental positions) with the key tone in the soprano produces a *perfect authentic cadence*; the same chord progression with the third or fifth of the tonic chord in the melody (or first inversion) produces the *imperfect authentic cadence.* It should be added that cadences usually are found on the accented part of the measure.

## HARMONY

**The dominant seventh.** Sing the following melody, observing the chord tones found in the bracketed measures:

**EX. 6-1**

As may be observed, the skips are all on the dominant, plus an additional third above the fifth, or *E, G♯, B, D.* It will be remembered that a three-tone chord is called a triad and is built by adding a third and fifth on alternate staff degrees above the root. A four-tone chord, as in Ex. 6-1 above, built in a similar manner, is called a *seventh-chord,* since seven degrees of the staff are embraced between the root and the highest tone, *E, F♯,G♯, A, B, C♯,D.* Since this chord of the sev-

$$1 \quad 2 \quad 3 \quad 4 \quad 5 \quad 6 \quad 7$$

enth is built on the dominant of the scale, it is called the dominant-seventh, $V_7$. It is often referred to as the seventh of the staff degree on which it originates, in the example above, the *E;* in other words, the $E_7$.

The dominant-seventh, like the dominant, is one of the most important chords in music and is often used as a substitute. When the four tones are sounded together, the total effect is that of anticipation or expectancy, a quality which results from the combination of active tones contained.[1] This combination of active tones is classified as *dissonant,* and its active or expectant tendency may be satisfied by moving to inactive tones. This movement of active tones of the dominant-seventh to the rest, or *consonant*[2] tones of the tonic, may be heard by play-

[1] See Chapter 3, p. 24.
[2] See Chapter 14, p. 170.

ing the last two measures of Ex. 6-1 above. The dominant-seventh as it occurs in the key of *C* is shown below in its four positions:

**EX.** 6-2

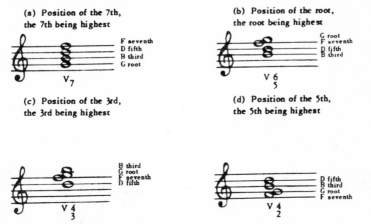

The student should observe the figures used in connection with the dominant-seventh as they are employed with all four-tone chords. At (*b*) the six and five identify the root (*G*) and seventh (*F*); at (*c*) the four and three designate the root (*G*) and seventh (*F*); and at (*d*) the four and two identify the third (*B*) and the root (*G*).

**EX.** 6-3

Passing and Neighboring Tones

(Other than those given for the dominant)

### RHYTHM

**Compound duple meter.** In our Melodies for Singing we have experienced duple, triple, and quadruple meters, all simple meters. We are now ready to consider a compound meter, the compound duple.[3] The conductor's beat pattern for this meter is shown in Ex. 6-4.

Sing Ex. 6-5, using the conductor's beat pattern:

Because this is a relatively slow-moving melody, we are able to feel each beat or count individually, and the conductor usually indicates each according to the conductor's beat pattern below. The pulses are in groups of three, with two groups to each measure, and an accent on the first

[3] See Chapter 2, p. 12.

## EX. 6-4

Compound Duple Meter

$$\frac{6}{8} \text{ or } \frac{6}{4} \text{ or } \frac{6}{16}$$

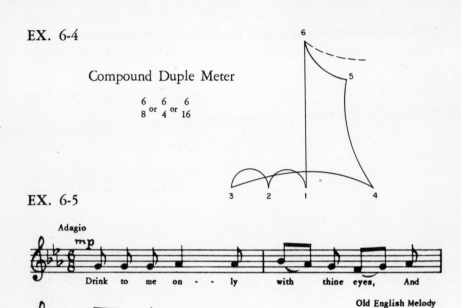

## EX. 6-5

Adagio

*mp*

Drink to me on - - ly   with   thine   eyes,   And

Old English Melody

I   will   pledge   with   mine

of each group. In contrast to the slow tempo above, sing the following, using the conductor's pattern again:

## EX. 6-6

Allegro M.M. $\dotminim$=72

*f*

English Melody

At so rapid a pace, the student probably found it impossible to move his hand quickly enough to indicate individual beats. Yet the pulsations were definitely in groups of threes, and no doubt a tendency was felt to tap the foot at the beginning of each group where the accent is found. Now sing the melody again, using only two beats in each measure. Observe that the beat fell either on a dotted quarter, which is equivalent to three eighth notes, or at the beginning of groups of three eighth notes. We may conclude from this experience that the conductor employs only two beats to the measure [4] in rapid tempos of compound

[4] For the conductor's pattern for duple meter, see Chapter 2, p. 12. For additional suggestions on the fundamentals of conducting, see Appendix B.

duple meter, and that one beat is given to each dotted quarter note or its equivalent. Note that the metronomic marking in Ex. 6-6 indicates that the tempo is at 72 dotted quarter notes per minute. Rapid tempos in compound meters are sometimes indicated at the beginning of the music in this manner.

## MELODIES FOR SINGING AND DICTATION

The following melodies contain examples of the melodic use of the tones of the dominant-seventh and examples in compound duple meter.

### MELODIES FOR SINGING

The Little Dustman    BRAHMS

Cradle Song    BRAHMS

Swedish Folk Song

If With All Your Hearts    From Elijah    MENDELSSOHN

French Folk Song

Hunting Song BUCCALOSSI

A Life on the Ocean Wave RUSSELL

Nearer My God To Thee MASON

Ah, I Have Sighed To Rest Me From Il Trovatore VERDI

I'm Going Away  BRAHMS

Fugue From Well Tempered Clavichord  BACH

## MELODIES FOR DICTATION

1 Presto — Old Song

2 Moderato — Tyrolese Folk Song

3 Presto — Swedish Folk Song

4 Moderato — Russian Folk Song

5 Allegretto — SUSSMAYER

74

## SUGGESTIONS FOR FURTHER STUDY

Observe the tempos of several compositions from the classical and modern periods.

Write the dominant-seventh chord in all major keys on the work sheet. Play them, and listen to the total effect and expectant tendency of this combination of active tones.

Identify the half and authentic cadences in the above Melodies for Singing.

Find examples of the perfect authentic cadences in the above melodies.

Examine the following imperfect cadences: No. 17, p. 103 (dictation); No. 14, p. 115; No. 11, p. 125; No. 3, p. 135; No. 5, p. 148.

Play the tonic and dominant-seventh chord progressions, Appendix A, No. 4, in all keys.

## WORK SHEET

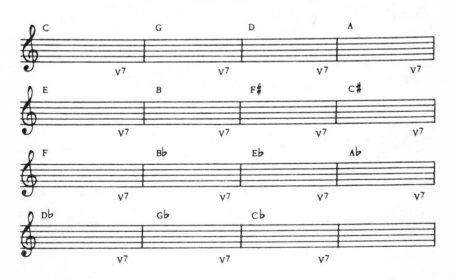

# • 7 •

# The Minor Scale

## *RUDIMENTS*

**The major and minor mode.** Play and sing the following familiar melody:

**EX. 7-1**

We Three Kings

The contrast between *A* and *B* above results from the use of two different *modes*, *A* being in the *minor mode*, seeming to have *E* as its key center, and *B* being in the *major mode,* tending to center around *G*. The contrast is, further, the result of the use of a different order of whole and half steps (to be treated more fully in Chapter 8) employed in the scales belonging to each of the modes. It should be noted that the key signature remains the same for both modes.

We have been using the term *mode* in its specific musical sense; it also has the more general meaning of *style* or *manner.* In a sense, this broader meaning also applies to the example above; that is, *A* seems to be in one manner or style and *B* in another. In our further discussions, however, the term will be used in its specific sense as defined above.

These two modes are used in music today for historical reasons. Because of their original association and the confusion over key signatures, the relationship of the two modes has been a controversial subject. There are basic facts concerning the two modes, however, on which all theorists agree. These facts and theories will be treated in this and in the following chapter.

The relative minor scale. For further observations concerning the modes, let us construct a scale from the key centers of the *A* and *B* parts of Example 7-1 above.

EX. 7-2

It will be noted that these two scales have a common signature and employ the same tones; the scales, however, begin at a different place and on a different key tone—which means, of course, that they are different keys, the first called *E* minor and the second *G* major. When this is true of any major and minor scales, they are said to be relative.[1] *E* minor is said to be the relative minor of *G* major, and *G* major, the relative major of *E* minor. Two further observations may be made: namely, (1) that the key center for the minor is found three degrees, comprising three half steps, below the major key center, and conversely, the key center for the major is found three degrees, comprising three

---

[1] Theorists differ as to the particular syllables used in singing the minor scale. Since this is true, the two possible sets of syllables are given here. Regardless of which set of syllables is used, the object is to hear and to sing the minor mode accurately. See the next chapter for justification for *do* as the key tone of the minor.

half steps, above the minor key center; (2) that the name of the major key is the same as the third tone of the minor scale.

Now let us construct these scales in the same setting as they originally appeared historically. The student should note that they also have a common signature and employ the same tones, but begin on a different key tone, and that the minor scale begins three degrees and three half steps below the major.

**EX. 7-3**

The minor scale, unlike the major, exists in a variety of forms. The historical form used above is known as the *modal, natural,* or *pure* form of the minor scale. Note, however, that it does not have a leading tone, or half step, between 7 and 8. In order to obtain one, and thus definitely strengthen the effect of the key tone, it is necessary to raise the pitch of the seventh step (g) one half tone to g♯ . Note that this change makes the scale progressions 7-8 or 8-7 in *A* minor correspond to those in *A* major, thus:

**EX. 7-4**

This is known as the *harmonic* form of the minor scale because it is the one most frequently used in harmony.

In order to avoid the awkward melodic interval resulting from this change—the step and a half now found between the sixth and seventh degrees—it is necessary in the ascending scale to raise the pitch of the sixth step (*f*) one half tone to *f* sharp—thus making the upper tetrachord (5-6-7-8) identical with that of *A* major. However, in the descending scale the natural form of the minor scale is used (*a-g-f-e*) as in Ex. 7-3. These two variants are known as the *melodic* form of the minor scale. (See Ex. 7-5 on following page.)

The symbols used on *G* and *F* are known as *naturals.* Such a character is used to cancel a sharp or a flat and thus to restore a note

**EX. 7-5**[2]

| la | ti | do | re | mi | fi | si | la | la | so | fa | mi | re | do | ti | la |
|----|----|----|----|----|----|----|----|----|----|----|----|----|----|----|----|
| 1  | 2  | 3  | 4  | 5  | 6  | 7  | 8  | 8  | 7  | 6  | 5  | 4  | 3  | 2  | 1  |

to its staff pitch. In order to raise the sixth and seventh steps in some of the keys, it is necessary to use a double sharp ( ✕· ) when the key signature designates a sharp on these degrees. The double sharp causes a degree on which a sharp has already been placed to represent a pitch one half step higher. A single sharp is used to restore a degree having a double sharp back to its staff pitch. On degrees which have been lowered by a flat in the key signature, it will be necessary to use the natural to cause them to represent a pitch one half step higher.

To summarize, we have three forms of the minor scale: the *natural,* the *harmonic,* and the *melodic.* Of these, the harmonic is the most important, since it is the basis for construction of the principal chords in the minor key. Its lowered third and sixth become the third in the tonic and subdominant chords, and the raised seventh becomes the third of the dominant chord, as will be seen in the chapters which follow.

**The period.** The average eight measure melody seems to fall into two parts or phrases of four measures each, the two being closely related; the first phrase seems to ask a question, and the second to answer it. The two are called, respectively, the *antecedent* and the *consequent.* The end of the antecedent is usually marked by some member of the dominant chord, although the imperfect authentic cadence may be used instead. The consequent usually ends with the perfect authentic cadence, though it also may end with the imperfect authentic cadence. The particular arrangement of phrases suggested by the discussion above is called a *period,* and it is sometimes referred to as the complete musical sentence. The following melodies illustrate this form: No. 4, p. 29; No. 8, p 43; No. 17, p. 44; No. 1, p. 69.

## HARMONY

**The tonic chord in minor.** We now turn to a consideration of the

---

[2] The student must not conclude from this presentation that the sixth and seventh are always raised in the ascending form and lowered in the descending. The upper tetrachord of the minor scale is variable, depending upon the harmonic background. See dictation melody No. 5, p. 86.

melodic use of the tones of the minor scale, and specifically to the tones of the chord founded on the first tone of the minor scale. Since the triad is built on the first tone, it is called the tonic chord. Like other triads, it is constructed by adding a third and fifth above the root, using alternate letters of the staff. It is shown below in the key of *A* minor in its three positions:

EX. 7-6

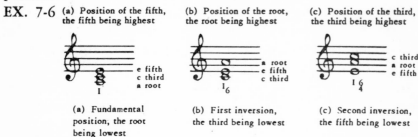

(a) Position of the fifth, the fifth being highest

(b) Position of the root, the root being highest

(c) Position of the third, the third being highest

(a) Fundamental position, the root being lowest

(b) First inversion, the third being lowest

(c) Second inversion, the fifth being lowest

As you play these tones together, note that the effect is different from that of the tonic chord in the major key; the reason is that the interval of the third of the tonic in minor is one half step smaller than that of the tonic in major. This will be explained more fully in Chapter 8.

Passing and neighboring tones of the tonic chord in A minor:
EX. 7-7

## RHYTHM

**The subdivided beat.** For a new experience in rhythm, sing the following melody, observing the use of the sixteenth notes (Ex. 7-8). It is evident in this example that the quarter note (the note receiving the beat) has been divided into eighths, and in some cases the eighths further divided into sixteenths. This may be seen by an examination

## EX. 7-8

of the first measure, from which it is apparent that the two eighth notes, as well as the four sixteenths, are performed during the time equivalent of one beat. The two sixteenths following the dotted quarter note in measures 5, 6, 7 (bracketed) are, of course, divisions of an eighth note and are performed in that time value. Sing the melody again, using the conductor's beat pattern, and observe the feeling produced by the groupings of sixteenth notes.

### MELODIES FOR SINGING AND DICTATION

The following melodies contain examples of the melodic use of chord tones of the tonic triad in minor and of the subdivided beat.

### MELODIES FOR SINGING[3]

---

[3] For signatures of minor keys see Chapter 9, Ex. 9-1.

Russian Folk Song

Russian Folk Song

Hungarian Melody

French Folk Song

## MELODIES FOR DICTATION

## SUGGESTIONS FOR FURTHER STUDY

Write the relative minor scale of all major keys in bass and treble, using the three forms of the minor scale.[4] After writing the key signature of the major key, write the minor scale, beginning on the third degree below the major key tone. This gives the natural form. Now raise the seventh tone to give the harmonic form, and finally raise both the sixth and seventh to obtain the melodic form. In descending, use the natural form. Play and sing these scales many times as you carefully observe the positions of 1, 3, 5, and 8.

Write and sing the following melody in the keys of *E, G, B,* and *D* minor.

Write the tonic chord in its three positions in the minor keys. Play them, listening to the total effect.

Play the tonic chord, Appendix A, No. 5, in all minor keys.

## WORK SHEET

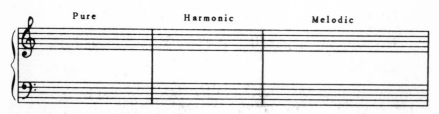

[4] See Chapter 9, p. 106.

# • 8 •

# The Minor Scale
## (Continued)

### RUDIMENTS

**The tonic minor scale.** Play the following example from the Beethoven Piano Sonata Op. 14, No. 2:

**EX. 8-1**

The key signature for this passage is *G*, but our ears tell us that the mode is minor rather than major. Evidently, then, Beethoven has changed the mode without changing the key—simply by lowering the third of the scale ($B$) and the sixth ($E$). This may be clearer if we examine the following example:

EX. 8-2

Both of these scales are constructed from $G$, but the first is the major and the second the minor scale. The change of mode was accomplished, then, by lowering the third and sixth degrees of the major scale by one half step. The result is the harmonic form of the minor scale. Had Beethoven desired the use of the pure form, he would have had to lower the seventh also. The three forms of the minor scale in $G$ appear thus:

EX. 8-3

Our comparison of structure indicates that the real difference between the major and the minor mode is that the minor third, sixth, and seventh are lower by one half step than they are in the major. As shown above, the lowering of the third, sixth, and seventh produces the natural form; the lowering of only the third and sixth, the harmonic; the lowering of the third, the melodic. The only consistent change here, of course, is the lowered third, since in minor the major form is often used for the upper portion or tetrachord of the scale. In other words, the upper portion of the scale is variable. Thus mode, or style or manner, refers more specifically to the interval pattern of the scale than to a change in key, as we shall see in a moment.

Had Beethoven desired to remain in the key of $G$ minor for a considerable length of time, he would have placed the flats in the key signature instead of writing them in each time they were needed. If this plan were followed, our three forms would appear thus:

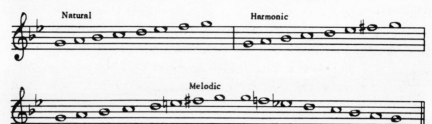

But whether the third, sixth, and seventh are lowered as needed or placed in the key signature, the key remains the same: in this case, G minor.

When the minor scale has the same tonic or key tone as the major, as in the Beethoven example, the scales are said to be *parallel*. Hence G minor is the parallel minor of G major and G major is the parallel major of G minor. Since the term *tonic* is sometimes applied to such scales because they have the same tonics, G minor is often called the tonic minor of G major, and conversely.

A review of the illustrations used in this and the preceding chapter suggests broadly the manner in which composers employ the major and minor modes. Whereas Part A of "We Three Kings" (see Ex. 7-1, p. 77) is in the key of E minor, Part B or the chorus is in the key of G major. This was possible under the same key signature since the two scales contained the same tones. In the Beethoven example (see Ex. 8-1, p. 92) however, where the major mode is changed to the minor, alterations of the scale steps were necessary, since these are not represented by the same key signature. In the use of the two modes, then, the composer has the following choices: (1) major key, (2) its relative minor, and (3) the parallel or tonic minor.

In order to lower the third, sixth, or seventh degrees when these have already been lowered by a flat in the key signature, it is necessary to use a double flat (♭♭) to effect a pitch one half step lower. To restore a degree where a double flat has been employed to its original single flat status, a single flat is used.

**Parallel and contrasting construction of the period.** When the initial portion of the consequent phrases of a period is an exact repetition of the first part of the antecedent, a period is said to be in *parallel construction*. The student should study the following melodies as examples of periods in parallel construction: No. 4, p. 29; No. 10, p. 30; No. 8,

p. 43; No. 10, p. 43; No. 15, p. 72; No. 4, p. 97; No. 1, p. 123; and No. 10, p. 149.

When the consequent phrase is melodically—and, sometimes, rhythmically—in contrast to the antecedent phrase, the period is in *contrasting construction.* The following melodies illustrate this: No. 17, p. 44; No. 1, p. 69; No. 16, p. 72; No. 12, p. 85; No. 15, p. 126; No. 3, p. 147.

## HARMONY

The dominant chord in the minor key has for its root the fifth tone of the key. The third and fifth are added on alternate staff degrees in the key of *A* minor, as shown below:

**EX. 8-5**

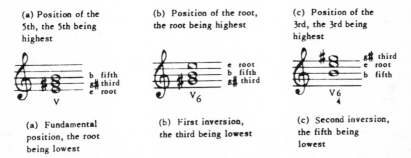

(a) Position of the 5th, the 5th being highest

(b) Position of the root, the root being highest

(c) Position of the 3rd, the 3rd being highest

(a) Fundamental position, the root being lowest

(b) First inversion, the third being lowest

(c) Second inversion, the fifth being lowest

Special attention must be called to the raised third of this chord. As was stated in Chapter 7, in harmony the harmonic form of the minor scale is used. In this form, it will be recalled, the seventh tone of the scale is raised. Since in the key of *A* minor, *G* is the seventh tone of the scale, and is, of course, the third of the dominant chord, it must be raised. In fact, the dominant triad in the minor is the same as the dominant chord in the parallel major—that is, the chord is the same in *A* major and *A* minor.

**EX. 8-6**     Passing and Neighboring Tones

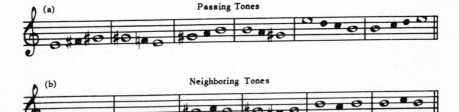

(a)     Passing Tones

(b)     Neighboring Tones

# RHYTHM

For a new experience in rhythm, sing the following melody:

EX. 8-7

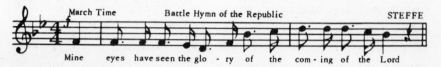

If we analyze this dotted-eighth-sixteenth rhythm, we find that the combined value of this combination of tones is equal to one quarter or one beat. By using the tie we can get a clearer picture of what actually takes place within the beat: ♪ ♪ ♪ ♪. In other words, the dotted-eighth length contains three sixteenths, which leaves only one sixteenth for the final portion of the beat.

## MELODIES FOR SINGING AND DICTATION

The following melodies contain the melodic use of the dominant chord tones in minor, as well as examples of the dotted eighth-sixteenth rhythm.

### MELODIES FOR SINGING

97

French Carol

Morris Dance Tune

99

100

Song of the Bird-Catcher   From The Magic Flute   MOZART

19  Moderato

Swedish Folk Song

20  Andante

Dearest Name   From Rigoletto   VERDI

## MELODIES FOR DICTATION

1 Andante   German Melody   Arr. BRAHMS  2 Andante

## SUGGESTIONS FOR FURTHER STUDY

Convert each of the major scales into a minor by lowering the third, sixth, and seventh tones.

Write the tonic chord in the major keys; convert each to a minor tonic chord by lowering the third. Play the major and then the minor, listening to the contrasting effects.

Sing the melodies in minor keys found in Melodies for Singing again, noticing the apparent change of mode from minor to major, then from major to minor.

Play the tonic and dominant chord progressions, Appendix A, No. 6, in all minor keys.

Examine several of your favorite compositions for examples of the three forms of the minor scale. Note the upper tetrachords, particularly the raised sixth and seventh in descending passages in No. 11 of the Bach Two-Part Inventions.

## WORK SHEET

# • 9 •

# Review of Major and Minor Keys

## RUDIMENTS

Relationship of scales, keys, and chords. The key signature of

**EX. 9-1**

all the major and minor keys and the tonic chord of each is given in Ex. 9-1. The student should become thoroughly familiar with each.

It was shown in Chapter 5 that the scales which immediately precede and follow a given scale are known as attendant or related scales, and that the scales of *F* and *G* major were closely related to that of *C* major. The relative minors, when they are added to *F, C,* and *G* major scales, are also in very close relation to the key of *C*. The attendant scales, with the more technical terms applied to such relationship, are shown below:

**EX. 9-2**

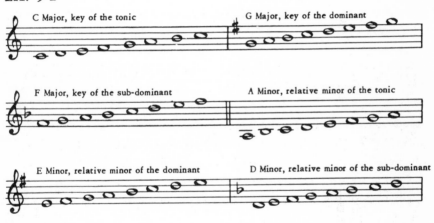

The same relationship also exists between a given minor scale and its attendant scales, as shown below and on the following page.

**EX. 9-3**

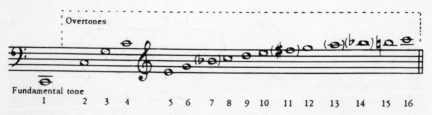

G major, relative major of the dominant    F major, relative major of the sub-dominant

So far our consideration of the relationship existing between scales, keys, and chords has not touched on the fundamental and significant reason for its existence. In Chapter 1 it was noted that the tones of the scale were related by natural laws of sound; in other words, they are based upon the physical fact that a vibrating body, such as a string, produces a series of sounds called *overtones* or *harmonics,* all of which exist in fixed ratio to the *fundamental tone* produced by the vibrating body.

Let us consider for a moment what happens when a string vibrates. Actually, it vibrates both as a whole and in segments. When such a string is touched at its midpoint, the two parts, being one-half as long, will vibrate twice as fast, producing a sound an octave above the pitch of the full length string. If the string is divided into three equal parts, the tone for each will be a twelfth above the original; if divided into four equal parts, the tone will be that of the double octave. And so on.

Example 9-4 shows great *C* as the fundamental and its accompanying overtones. In any instance in which the overtones are designated, the fundamental tone is called the first *partial*; the first overtone, or octave above the fundamental, the second partial, and the second overtone, the third partial, and so on. Note the numbering of partials in Ex. 9-4. The use of numbers provides a means of calculating the ratios of the partials to each other mathematically. For example, the vibratory ratio of the octave is 1:2—that is, the vibrations of the upper tone of the octave are twice those of the lower; the ratio of the fifth is 2:3; etc.

EX. 9-4

Overtones

Fundamental tone
1    2    3    4    5  6    7  8  9  10   11   12   13   14   15   16

Two observations may be made. (1) The second overtone (*G*) stands in very close relationship to the fundamental (*C*) because it is the first pitch differing in letter from the fundamental. The relationship of these

108

two tones (*C-G*) suggests the perfect fifth (see p. 131) as a basis of relationship between the tones of the major scale. (2) Parentheses have been placed around certain notes. This is done to indicate that, actually, the staff representations are not accurate indications of the true overtone pitches. This suggests that our system of tuning is a compromise between the natural harmonic relations and the need to make available twelve equal divisions within the octave.

The student may hear some of these upper partials or overtones by experimenting at the piano. For example, if he will raise the damper on small *c* by depressing the key, and strike and release great *C* (the octave below), the first overtone (the octave above) will be heard. In a similar manner, depress *G* and strike great *C*, and the second overtone (*G*) may be heard. In the same fashion, depress *e*¹, strike great *C*, and listen for the fourth overtone (*e*¹). It will be noted that the first overtone, the octave above great *C,* may be considered as a duplication of the fundamental. The second overtone is the twelfth, or *G* (which, for our purpose, may be reduced to the fifth).[1] This interval, the fifth, or any two tones which lie a perfect fifth apart, are in the closest possible harmonic relationship. With the next overtone we again discover the octave, again a duplication. The fourth overtone, *e*¹, however, stands in the relationship of a major third to the fundamental. These first several overtones, as can be easily seen, are the very familiar members of the tonic chord in the key of *C*.

As stated in the preceding paragraph, the closest possible relationship exists between tones standing a perfect fifth apart. The same is true of the relationship existing between scales, chords, and keys founded upon tones which lie a perfect fifth apart. To the introductory observations already made on the apparent kinship between scales with common tetrachords, a further one should be made concerning the tones of the principal chords of the major key, I, IV, and V: namely, that the chord members of these triads are derived from the overtones produced when their roots are used as the fundamental tone.

EX. 9-5

[1] See Chapters 11 and 15 for information concerning intervals.

Note in Ex. 9-5 that $C$ is a perfect fifth above $F$, and $G$ a perfect fifth above $C$. As stated immediately above, chords built upon these closely related tones stand in the same relationship as the tones themselves. Furthermore, the chord members derived from the overtones produced by $F$, $C$, and $G$ as fundamentals are the tones of the scale and key of $C$.

## HARMONY

**The subdominant chord in minor.** The root of the subdominant chord in minor is found on the fourth tone of the scale, with its third and fifth on alternate degrees above. Shown below are its three positions in the key of $A$ minor:

**EX. 9-6**

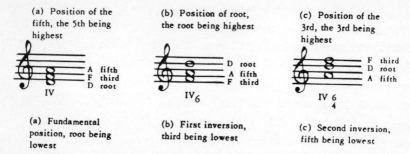

(a) Position of the fifth, the 5th being highest

(b) Position of root, the root being highest

(c) Position of the 3rd, the 3rd being highest

(a) Fundamental position, root being lowest

(b) First inversion, third being lowest

(c) Second inversion, fifth being lowest

The passing and neighboring tones are as follows:

**EX. 9-7**

(a)        Passing Tones

(b)        Neighboring Tones

## RHYTHM

**The dotted eighth and sixteenth in $\frac{6}{8}$ time.** Sing the following melody:

**EX. 9-8**

Adagio
pp
Silent Night
GRUBER

Si - - lent night !        Ho - - - ly night !

This rhythm, the dotted eighth followed by the sixteenth in $\frac{6}{8}$ time, differs from that found in the preceding chapter, where the quarter note was used as the beat, in that there the total time value of the two notes was one beat, whereas in the example above, the time value of the two notes is two beats. The result is triple groups in which unequal note values occur.

## MELODIES FOR SINGING AND DICTATION

The following melodies contain examples of the melodic treatment of the tones of the subdominant chord in minor and the dotted-eighth-sixteenth rhythm in compound duple meter.

### MELODIES FOR SINGING

Russian Folk Song

Russian Folk Song

Home To Our Mountains    From Il Trovatore   VERDI

² See page 145, Ex. 12-14 for explanation of the four-bar rest.

Old French Song

Spring Dreams SCHUBERT

[3] The small note is known as an acciaccatura, and should be sung as quickly as possible with the accent upon the principal note.

114

115

Clown's Song SCHUMANN

## MELODIES FOR DICTATION

## SUGGESTIONS FOR FURTHER STUDY

| Write the attendant scales of the keys of G, D, A, F, B♭, and E♭, at a in the Work Sheet.

Write the subdominant chord in the major keys. Convert each to a minor triad by lowering the third.

Play the tonic and subdominant chords, Appendix A, No. 7, in all minor keys.

## WORK SHEET

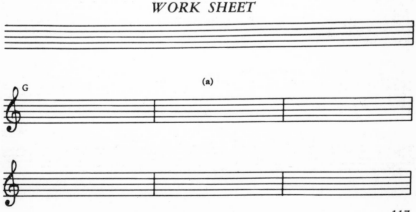

(a)

G

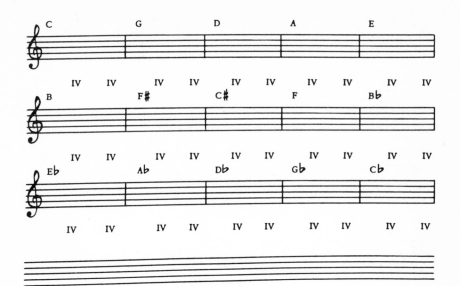

# · 10 ·

# Dynamics

**Degrees of sound-volume.** Of great importance to the expressive performance of music is its relative loudness and softness, or *dynamics*. The ability to recognize dynamic markings and to interpret them in terms of effective performance is as important as the ability to hear tones. By means of special words, abbreviations, and signs the composer is able to indicate the degree of dynamics he desires. A brief list of these follow:

Piano $p$ —softly

Forte $f$ —loudly

Forzando $fz$

Sforzando $sf, sfz$

Forzato $fz$  These words and signs indicate that a tone or a chord is to receive special stress or accent.

Sforzato $sf, sfz$

　or $>$ $\land$

Crescendo (cres. or ⤳ —gradually louder

Decrescendo (decresc. or ⤳ —gradually softer

Diminuendo (dim. or ⤳ —gradually softer

Amore—tenderness, affection

Bravura—boldness, spirit

Energia—energy, force

Espressione—expression, feeling

120

**Brio**—vigor, animation

**Fuoco**—fire, energy

**Passione**—passion, feeling

**Grazia**—grace, elegance

**Tenerezza**—tenderness, delicacy

**Dolce**—sweetly, softly

**Maestoso**—majestic, stately

**Pomposo**—pompously

**Sotto Voce**—subdued voice

These terms may be combined with others found in Chapter 6 dealing with tempo.

**The double period.** The *double period,* when regular, consists of four phrases, representing a combination of two single periods. In the same fashion that the antecedent and consequent phrases of an individual period depend on each other, the two periods of a double period are mutually dependent. The first phrase of the double period usually ends on the third or fifth tone of the scale (tonic chord), whereas the second phrase closes with a half cadence (dominant chord). The third phrase may end in a manner similar to that of the first phrase, but it often moves toward the subdominant chord. The fourth phrase, as may be expected, closes with the perfect authentic cadence. Examples of melodies in this form are as follows: p. 56, No. 3; p. 71, No. 10; p. 147, No. 1.

## HARMONY

**The dominant seventh in minor.** The *dominant seventh in minor* is built on the fifth tone of the scale. It, like any chord of the seventh, consists of four tones on alternate staff degrees. Since the three upper tones of the chord are active, they demand, when sounded together, a resolution to rest tones. The chord in its four positions is shown below and on the following page.

**EX. 10-1**

(a) Position of the 7th,
the 7th being highest

(b) Position of the root,
the root being highest

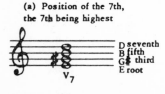

D seventh
B fifth
G♯ third
E root

V₇

(a) Fundamental position,
the root being lowest

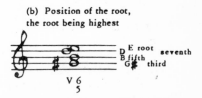

E root  seventh
B fifth
G♯ third

V 6
5

(b) First inversion, the third
being lowest

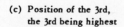

(c) Position of the 3rd,
the 3rd being highest

(d) Position of the 5th,
the 5th being highest

(c) Second inversion,
the fifth being lowest

(d) Third inversion, the seventh
being lowest

The passing and neighboring tones (other than those given for the dominant, Chapter 8) are as follows:

EX. 10-2

## RHYTHM

**The triplet.** Sing the following well known melody:

EX. 10-3

Notice the groups of three notes joined together by a curved line and designated by the figure three. These are known as *triplets* and are executed in the time of two tones of like value. In "Juanita" the three eighth-note groups are sung in the time equivalent of two eighth notes. The first note of the group is accented.

Triplets may be formed of notes of any length, or of a combination of notes and rests, as in the following:

EX. 10-4

## MELODIES FOR SINGING AND DICTATION

The following melodies contain examples of the dominant seventh chord in minor and triplets.

# MELODIES FOR SINGING

1. Allegro

*mf* I (g) Minor    V⁷    I    V

English Melody

I    V⁷    I    V⁷    I

2. Allegro con Brio

*ff*    I (f) Minor    I    V⁷    I

I    I    V⁷    I

Refrain, Audacious Tar from H.M.S. Pinafore, SULLIVAN

3. Moderato

*mf* I (g) Minor    V⁷    I    V

I    V⁷    I    V⁷    I    I    V

Norwegian Folk Song

V    I    IV    I    V⁷    I

4. Un Poco Piu Lento

*p*    I (a♭) Minor    V⁷    I

I    V⁷

123

Can I Survive This Overbearing  from H.M.S. Pinafore  SULLIVAN

Death of Ase  from Peer Gynt Suite  GRIEG

Things Are Seldom What They Seem  from H.M.S. Pinafore  SULLIVAN

To The Waiter  SCHUMANN

Molly's Hoop  Old English Melody

Three Merry Men of Kent    English Melody

Pilgrim's Chorus   from Tannhauser   WAGNER

Serenade   SCHUBERT

On The Immortal Height *from Attila* VERDI

## MELODIES FOR DICTATION

## SUGGESTIONS FOR FURTHER STUDY

Write the dominant seventh chord in the minor keys (see Chapter 8, p. 95 concerning the raised third).

Examine several of your favorite compositions for examples of the triplet and dynamics.

Play the tonic and dominant seventh chord progressions, Appendix A, No. 8, in all minor keys.

## WORK SHEET

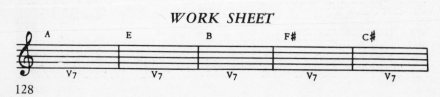

# • 11 •

# Major, Perfect and Minor Intervals

*RUDIMENTS*

Classification of intervals. The difference in pitch between two tones, as we have already learned, is called an interval. In Ex. 11-1 below are two intervals that the student should play on the piano:

EX. 11-1

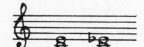

Two observations may be made with regard to this example which will help us to understand more clearly the nature of intervals. (1) Although there is a similarity between these intervals in that each involves three degrees of the staff—C, D, E—they actually sound differently when played on the piano. (2) The difference in the sounds of these intervals results from the fact that they are different in size; that is, each contains a different number of half steps: the first one, C to E, four half steps; the second, C to E♭ three. On the basis of these observations it may be stated that intervals are classified in two ways: according to the number of staff degrees involved and according to the number of half steps contained. The first gives us the general name of the interval and the second the particular name. The intervals in Ex. 11-1 are thirds, embracing as they do three degrees of the staff—C, D, and E. This is their general name. Their particular name is determined by counting the number of half steps contained. However, a more con-

130

venient method for arriving at their particular name is normally used, the basis of which is the application of the major scale. For example, an interval from the key tone of the major scale to any other tone of the major scale is either *major* or *perfect*. Examine the following:

EX. 11-2

**Major and perfect intervals.** Note that the interval from 1 to 2 of any major scale is a major second; from 1 to 3, a major third; from 1 to 6, a major sixth; from 1 to 7, a major seventh; from 1 to 9, a major ninth; and similarly that the interval from 1 to 1 is a perfect prime; from 1 to 4, a perfect fourth; from 1 to 5, a perfect fifth; and from 1 to 8, a perfect octave.[2] *Note*: this should be committed to memory, for it will be used as the basis for calculating all other intervals.

It may be stated as a general rule that the particular name of any interval is determined by its relation to the major scale, by whether the upper tone of the interval occurs as a tone of the major scale, or whether the upper tone of the interval is higher or lower than the corresponding tone of the major scale.

**Minor intervals.** The minor intervals have the same general name as the major—that is, they have the same number of degrees of the staff—but since they are one half step smaller, the upper tone of the interval being lower than the corresponding tone in the major scale, the particular name is different. The minor intervals with their particular names are illustrated in the following: [3]

EX. 11-3

**Melodic and harmonic intervals; major and minor chords.** An

[1] The unison (Latin: *unus sonus,* one sound) is really not an interval, but is considered as such for convenience in classification. Another name for it is the *prime*.

[2] See p. 170.

[3] The student must not conclude that only minor intervals are found in the minor scale. It will be recalled that the upper tetrachord of the minor scale is variable depending on the form used.

interval is melodic when the two tones are heard in succession. Examine the following example:

EX. 11-4

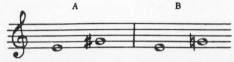

These are, of course, thirds, even though they are not sounded simultaneously. Now using our general rule we can also determine their particular names. Considering *E* as the key tone of the *E*-major scale, then *G♯* in *A* above is the third tone of the *E*-major scale, and therefore a major third. In *B*, consider *E* again as the key tone of the *E*-major scale. In this case, however, *G* is smaller by one half step than the third tone of the *E*-major scale, and the interval is, therefore, a minor third.

An interval is harmonic when the tones are heard simultaneously. Since this phenomenon is quite common in chords, let us examine the harmonic intervals of chords we have studied in the past, for instance, the I, IV, V, and V₇ in the major and minor keys.

EX. 11-5

In the Tonic, the interval of *C* to *E* is a major third, that from *C* to *G*, a perfect fifth. The subdominant IV and the dominant V also have a major third and a perfect fifth: namely, *F* to *A* and *F* to *C* in the subdominant, and *G* to *B* and *G* to *D* in the dominant. Thus each chord contains the intervals of a major third and a perfect fifth. On the basis of the thirds contained, the lower third of the chords is a major third and the upper third a minor third. Any triad with these intervals is called a *major chord*.

Now let us consider the intervals of these chords as they occur in *C*-minor:

EX. 11-6

To summarize:

Tonic: C to E♭  minor third; C to G, perfect fifth
Subdominant: F to A♭  minor third; F to C, perfect fifth
Dominant: G to B, major third; G to D, perfect fifth

132

Thus the I and IV chords contain the intervals of a minor third, and a perfect fifth. Considering the thirds, the lower third of the chord is minor, the upper third major. Any triad with these intervals is a *minor chord*. The V chord, in *C* above, has a major third rather than a minor third, though it does have the perfect fifth. The V chord, in other words, is the same as it is in the major key.

The dominant seventh, like the dominant, is invariable; that is, its intervals are the same in both the major and minor key. The dominant seventh is shown below in *C*-major and *C*-minor:

EX. 11-7

*G* to *B,* is a major third; *G* to *D,* a perfect fifth; *G* to *F,* a minor seventh.

## HARMONY

**Review of harmony.** In the preceding chapters we have studied the principal triads (I, IV, and V) in both the major and minor key, as well as the dominant seventh chord in the major and minor key. We may now briefly review these chords and their interval content:

1. A triad is formed by adding a third and fifth to a given tone called the root.

2. Any member of the chord may occur as the highest tone of the chord.

3. Any member of the chord may occur as the lowest tone of the chord.

4. If the third of a triad is major and the fifth is perfect, the chord is major. The tonic, dominant, and subdominant triads in the major key are major chords.

5. If the third of a triad is minor and the fifth is perfect, the chord is minor. The tonic and subdominant chords in the minor key are minor; the dominant, on the other hand, is major.

6. By adding a third to the dominant triad we get the tones of the dominant seventh chord. The intervals of this chord in both the major and minor key are a major third, a perfect fifth, and a minor seventh.

## RHYTHM

**Compound triple meter.** When there are nine units of rhythm in a measure, they fall into three groups of three units each, forming a *compound triple* meter having the effect of a simple triple meter such as $\frac{3}{4}$ employing triplets. The accents fall on the first of each triple group, or on beats one, four, and seven. If the tempo is rapid, there will be only three beats in each measure because each group of three beats is felt as one beat. This is usually known as compound triple meter. An interesting experiment may be made by writing a measure of "Juanita," first in its proper $\frac{3}{4}$ meter, then in $\frac{9}{8}$ time, thus:

EX. 11-8

EX. 11-9

In the first representation, each quarter note or its equivalent gets a beat; in the second, the dotted quarter note or equivalent. Actually, to the ear they are the same.

## MELODIES FOR SINGING AND DICTATION

As may have been observed, no new chord was introduced in this chapter. Instead the stress was on intervals as they occur between the successive tones in melody. The student will find intervals, especially of the wide variety, which he has not encountered heretofore. The melodies also contain examples in compound triple meter.

### MELODIES FOR SINGING

On Wings of Music  MENDELSSOHN

3  Moderato

Lithuanian Folk Song  4  Andante

From Symphony No. 6  HAYDN

5  Largo

Behold, And See If There Be Any Sorrow  From The Messiah  HANDEL

6  Andante

Thou Shalt Break Them  From The Messiah  HANDEL

With Joy Th' Impatient Husbandman  From The Seasons  HAYDN

O God, Have Mercy  From St. Paul  MENDELSSOHN

136

Where'er You Walk  From Semele  HANDEL

**10  Andante**

Look Down On Us From Heaven  From Elijah  MENDELSSOHN

**11  Moderato**

Beautiful Dreamer  FOSTER

**12  Andante**

From St. Cecilia Mass  GOUNOD

**13  Andantino**

Over The Bright Blue Sea   From H.M.S. Pinafore SULLIVAN

The Message  BRAHMS 15  Lento

Not a Breath in Heaven Stirs   BRAHMS 16  Lento

Lamentation  MOUSSORGSKY 17  Andante   Have You Heard of a Frolicsome Ditty?  PEPUSCH

## MELODIES FOR DICTATION

He More Knightly Than The Noblest  SCHUMANN

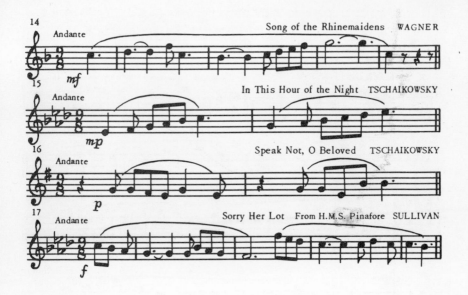

## SUGGESTIONS FOR FURTHER STUDY

Identify the intervals on the work sheet, giving both the general and the specific names. Play each tone of the interval in succession and then simultaneously, listening to the effect.

Write the I, IV, V and $V_7$ chords in the keys of *G* major and *G* minor. Indicate the intervals of each chord. Play them, listening to the total effect.

Identify the melodic intervals in melodies 1, 3, and 4 in Melodies for Singing.

Play the chord progressions, Appendix A, No. 9, in all keys.

## WORK SHEET

G Major

| I | IV | V | V7 |

G Minor

| I | IV | V | V7 |

# · 12 ·

# Additional Symbols Used in Music

## RUDIMENTS

**Miscellaneous signs.** The *fermata* is the Italian term for the sign
⌒ , in English usually called a *hold*. It signifies that the note or
rest over which it is placed is to be prolonged beyond its natural duration. There is no rule concerning the length of the increased duration,
this being left to the judgment of the performer. The fermata is also
placed over a measure bar or a double bar to indicate a short period of
silence.

The slur, introduced in an earlier chapter relative to its use in singing, is also used extensively in instrumental music to indicate a special
phrasing effect. When it is placed over or under a group of notes, they
are to be performed with the smoothness more commonly expressed by
the term *legato*. Play the following examples, observing the use of this
important phrasing device.

**EX. 12-1**

**EX. 12-2**

**EX. 12-3**

Dots over or under the notes indicate an effect just the opposite of that indicated by the slur or phrase mark—indicating, rather, that the tones are to be detached. *Note*:

**EX. 12-4**

Tones so indicated are to be made shorter and to be separated by periods of silence, as though they were played or sung as follows:

**EX. 12-5**

Sometimes the slur and the *staccato,* are combined:

**EX. 12-6**

The tones are to be detached, but with briefer periods of silence, thus:

**EX. 12-7**

This is known as *mezzo staccato,* or *portato.*

The *arpeggio sign* ⦃ , placed before a chord, suggests that the tones, beginning with the lowest, are to be played as a rapid succession of tones. The result is a harp-like effect.

EX. 12-8

The octave transposition sign, *8va,* followed by a dotted line, signifies that the notes are to be played an octave higher than written. The notes so affected are those embraced by the sign itself and the line, thus:

EX. 12-9

Where the composer wishes the notes to be played an octave lower, in the bass, he uses the signs *8va bassa* or *8va sotta.* If the note is to be accompanied by its octave either above or below, the terms *Con 8va* or *All 8va* are placed above or below the note:

EX. 12-10

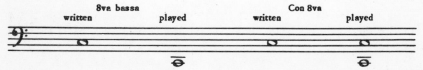

In orchestral music, one or more lines drawn through a stem of a note indicate that the note is to be repeated: a single line indicates the repetition is to be eighth notes, a double line, sixteenths.

EX. 12-11

The same shorthand device is also used for notes on different degrees of the staff.

EX. 12-12

A sign for the repetition of a group of notes in orchestral music is ⅍. Its use is illustrated in the following:

EX. 12-13

Silent measures in any musical score are indicated by the whole rest sign with a number placed above to indicate the number of measures to be silent.

EX. 12-14

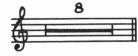

A number of methods are used where sections of music are to be repeated. The sign for the repetition of a whole section of a composition is a double perpendicular bar and a row of dots. For example:

EX. 12-15

If the repeated portion is to end differently from the first, it is indicated in the following manner:

EX. 12-16

Sometimes the term *Da Capo* (from the beginning, abbreviated *D.C.*) placed at the end of a section is used to indicate a repeat from the beginning. The term *D. C. al Fine* is also used. In this case, the repeated portion ends with the bar over which the word *Fine* again appears. The term *Dal Segno* (from the sign, abbreviated *D.S.*) appearing at the

145

end of a section directs the performer to repeat, beginning from a point marked by the sign: ·✗· The word *Fine* again marks the end of the repetition. The *coda* sign ⊕ used at some point in a repeated portion, indicates that a skip is to be made from that point to the coda or closing portion of the composition.

The use of the damper pedal on the piano is indicated by the abbreviation *Ped.,* and its use terminates with the appearance of the sign \*. The following signs are also used:

**EX.** 12-17

## HARMONY

**The supertonic chord.** We have learned that the principal chords of the major key are the tonic (I), the dominant (V), and the subdominant (IV). The major key also has chords called *secondary chords,* the names of which are the *supertonic* (II), the *mediant* (III), and the *submediant* (VI). All of these secondary triads are minor chords.

The most important of these triads is the supertonic (above tonic), formed on the second degree of the scale. It is used in fundamental position and in the first inversion, but rarely in the second inversion. It is shown below in the two positions in which it is most frequently found.

**EX.** 12-18

II    II₆

Its intervals are a minor third and a perfect fifth. The passing and neighboring tones are the same as for the IV in the minor key (except for the chromatically raised seventh of the minor scale), which may be found in Chapter 9, p. 110.

## RHYTHM

**Compound quadruple meter.** When there are 12 units of rhythm in a measure, they fall into four groups of three units each, forming a compound quadruple meter having the effect of a simple quadruple meter such as $\frac{4}{4}$ employing triplets. The accents fall on the first of each triple group, or on beats one, four, seven, and ten. If the tempo is rapid, the conductor's pattern calls for only four beats in each measure. This is usually known as *compound quadruple meter*.

Melody No. 21 in Melodies for Singing includes rhythmic problems of considerable complexity for the beginner. The first approach to feeling this rhythm is through counting twelve beats to the measure, each eighth note receiving one beat. With this approach, the sixteenth notes become equal divisions and the thirty-second notes equal subdivisions of the beat. The student should be cautioned to maintain a legato singing style. When these divisions are understood and felt, four beats to the measure should be used with particular attention being given to the note on which each beat occurs.

## MELODIES FOR SINGING AND DICTATION

The following melodies contain examples of the supertonic chord and of compound quadruple meter.

### MELODIES FOR SINGING

Oh, Praise The Lord  From Athalie  MENDELSSOHN

5 Allegro

Intermezzo, Op. 61 No. 5  MENDELSSOHN

6 Allegretto

148

17  Allegro Moderato

*mf*

Torments of Hate and Vengeance

From Lucia di Lammermoor  DONIZETTI  18  Andante Moto

*p* I          V6          IV

Charity  ROSSINI

I          V7          I

19  Largo

I Think of Thee  SCHUBERT

*f*

20  Larghetto

*mf*

Pastoral Symphony  From Messiah  HANDEL

## MELODIES FOR DICTATION

1  Allegro

German Folk Song

*f*

## SUGGESTIONS FOR FURTHER STUDY

Examine several of your favorite compositions for examples of the symbols presented in this chapter.

Examine an orchestral score for examples of symbols for repeated passages.

Identify the intervals on the work sheet. Play each tone of the interval, first successively, then simultaneously, listening to the effect.

Write the I, IV, V and V$_7$ chords in the keys of $F$ major and $F$ minor. Indicate the intervals of each chord. Play them, listening to the total effect.

Play the chord progressions, Appendix A, No. 10, in all keys.

# WORK SHEET

F Major                      F Minor

    I       IV       V       V7         I       IV       V       V7

# · 13 ·

# Elementary Musical Forms

## RUDIMENTS

**A review of form.** In each of the preceding chapters we have been dealing with, and giving emphasis to, the elements of *form*. Our first experience was with the orderly grouping of the strong and weak *accents* into measures. Later we observed that measures were grouped into phrases, and phrases into periods. Again, it was discovered that even the arrangement of rhythmic patterns within the phrase was evidence of order. The second major experience had to do with the grouping of *tones* into phrases. We observed that the antecedent and consequent phrases were united into a period by parallel and contrasting construction, and that two periods, when combined, formed the double period. Even the melodic movement, with its relationship to the chord, was thus suggestive of design. The third experience was with *harmony*. The chord changes usually occurred upon the accented part of the measure, and the particular type of cadence was determined by the use of a certain chord, or chords. Even the folk and art melodies within the preceding chapters suggest harmonic schemes.

Thus the three elements of music—rhythm, melody, and harmony —constitute the very essence of form, being elements so interdependent and so inseparably bound that it is difficult to think of one without the other. The folk and composed melodies, in their rhythmic and harmonic settings, bear witness of the symmetry, design, balance, and beauty of form.

**Plagal and deceptive cadences.** From our earlier study of cadence, it will be recalled that the half-cadence consisted of dominant harmonies at the close of a phrase; that the dominant to tonic progression, with the root of the chord in the melody, resulted in the perfect authentic cadence; and that the same harmonies (dominant to tonic) with the third or fifth of the chord in the melody brought about the imperfect authentic cadence.

There remain now but two new cadences for our consideration. The first of these consists of a subdominant to tonic progression, as found in the familiar church *amen*:

EX. 13-1

This is known as the *plagal cadence* and is often added as an extension of the phrase ending with the perfect authentic cadence. This is easily discernible in many hymns.

The second cadence to be considered is the *deceptive* or *interrupted* close. This occurs when the dominant or dominant seventh resolves to any unexpected chord. A good example is found in the Handel "Largo," where the dominant harmonies progress to the submediant (VI),[1] as shown below:

EX. 13-2

**Other form elements.** With this background, we are now ready to make further observations concerning form. First let us sing an interesting phrase from Verdi's "Il Trovatore":

1 See p. 159.

## EX. 13-3

Now contrast it with the following familiar melody from Mozart's "The Marriage of Figaro":

## EX. 13-4

It is quite evident that the composers of these two melodies have taken a group of three tones in a simple rhythmic pattern and repeated them, either at the same pitch or by sequence. This small group of tones, as we have already learned, is called a *figure* and is the smallest of musical ideas. The student will also find "When Love Is Kind," p. 150, No. 13, interesting from this standpoint.

Now sing this familiar melody from Dvorak's Symphony No. 5.

## EX. 13-5

Here again the composer has used a small group of tones, extending them into a well-balanced melody. Note that the repetitions are more varied than in Exs. 13-3 and 13-4. Note also that in measures 5, 6, 7, and 8, the composer has changed the direction of the third and altered the rhythm to give variety. We may conclude from these observations that *repetition*—exact or in sequence—*is one of the fundamental principles of form,* and that a phrase or even a longer passage is often developed from a very small group of tones.

**Binary form.** Sing the following melody:

EX. 13-6

French Folk Song

This folk song consists of two different melodic parts, each of which ends with the perfect cadence. But, though the two parts are different, they seem to belong together. Such combinations of parts unlike in melody, where the second part acts as a response to the first, are known as *binary* or *two-part* form, often designated as A-B form. Other examples are Melody No. 3, p. 135; No. 8, p. 70; and No. 1, p. 96.

**Ternary form.** Sing the following melody—"Old Folks at Home" by Stephen C. Foster.

EX. 13-7

Analyzing this melody, we find the following features:

( 1 ) The first phrase ends on the dominant chord to form the half-cadence.

( 2 ) The second phrase ends on the tonic preceded by the dominant to form the authentic cadence.

( 3 ) The first two phrases are identical except at the cadence.

( 4 ) The tone at the cadence (the dotted half) is longer than the preceding tones.

( 5 ) The cadence in each case falls on the strong part of the measure.

( 6 ) The third phrase is unlike the others.

( 7 ) The fourth phrase condenses the original thought by repeating only phrase two.

( 8 ) In this melody, A is a parallel period, and B and A are phrases.

From these observations it may be concluded that all phrases end with a cadence, that the cadence is often made more prominent by a long tone, and that it occurs on the accented part of the measure. Observations 6 and 7 suggest the basis of *ternary* or *three-part form,* often designated as *A-B-A.* According to Observation 6, the third phrase in Ex.

158

13-7 is a distinct digression from the original idea; according to Observation 7, the fourth phrase is a restatement or recapitulation of the original thought. The ternary form may be defined, then, as a statement, digression, and restatement of musical ideas. The length of each part in a simple ternary form may vary, but the basic design remains stable. Other examples of the *A-B-A* form are melodies No. 12, p. 43, No. 2, p. 96, and No. 3, p. 97.

*Note*: Although the ideas expressed in this chapter and its examples concern only the smallest of musical forms, they reveal the basic principles upon which the larger forms of music are also based.

## HARMONY

**The submediant chord.** The *submediant chord* is that secondary triad next in importance to the supertonic. Since its tones and intervals are the same as those of the tonic chord in the minor key, the student will encounter no difficulty in singing the melodies in this chapter. It is built on the sixth tone of the scale and often follows the dominant or the dominant seventh instead of the tonic. It is also used as a connecting link between the tonic and subdominant chords. Since the passing and neighboring tones of this chord are the same as for the tonic triad in the minor key (except for the chromatically raised seventh tone of the minor scale), the student is referred to them, Chapter 7, p. 81. The submediant chord is shown below in fundamental position and first inversion, the ways it is most frequently found.

EX. 13-8

VI    VI₆

## RHYTHM

**Syncopation.** *Syncopation* is a rhythmic phenomenon which results when the normal expected pulsation of meter, accent, and rhythm pattern is upset. As we have already learned, rhythm is based upon the combining of the beats into groups of two and three, having a regular recurring accent on the first beat of each group. The upsetting of the normal rhythm, which we call syncopation, is accomplished by shifting the stress to the normally weak accents. Note the following examples. At (a) the normal pulsation is upset by the tie which forces the accent

## EX. 13-9

to fall on the weak part of the measure. At (b) syncopation is brought about in two ways: first, by the quarter notes on E and C falling on the unaccented part of the beat, and second, by holding the eighth note over the measure bar into the strong accent. At (c) the regular pulsation of the meter is upset by the rests which occur on the strong part of measures 2, 4, and 6.

Syncopation also results from accenting an unaccented part of the measure, as Beethoven did in the Scherzo of the Eroica Symphony.

## EX. 13-10

The student will find interesting examples of syncopation in Chapter 12, melody No. 17, p. 151, and melody No. 20, p. 151.

## MELODIES FOR SINGING AND DICTATION

The following melodies contain examples of the chord tones of the submediant, and of syncopation.

## MELODIES FOR SINGING

160

The Lord's My Shepherd  HAVERGAL

Now Let Every Tongue Adore Thee  From Sleeper's Wake  BACH

Lord, Make Me to Know  From Requiem  BRAHMS

161

Lo, How a Rose   PRAETORIOUS

10 Allegro Moderato

Czechoslovakian Folk Song

11 Andante Molto

Moonlight and Roses   LEMARE

12 Andante

rit.

Highland Cradle Song   SCHUMANN

² There is a modulation to F sharp minor in the sixth measure of this melody.   163

# MELODIES FOR DICTATION

## SUGGESTIONS FOR FURTHER STUDY

Examine several of your favorite compositions for examples of the various cadences.

Listen for examples of repetition, exact or in sequence, in your favorite recordings.

Find examples of syncopation in a Bach, Beethoven, and Schumann composition.

Identify the intervals on the work sheet. Play the lower tone; sing the upper; test by playing each in succession. Play the lower tone again. Can you imagine the total effect if both tones were sounded simultaneously? Try it, and then test by playing.

Play the chord progressions, Appendix A, No. 11, in all major keys.

## WORK SHEET

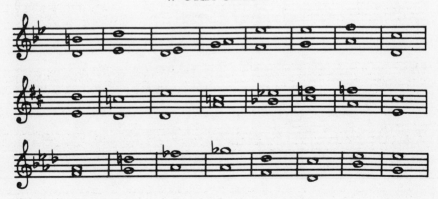

• 14 •

# The Chromatic Scale

### RUDIMENTS

**Construction of the chromatic scale.** Begin at Middle *C* and play successively all the white and black keys through an octave. This series of tones is known as the *chromatic* scale (Greek: *chroma*, color). It is built entirely upon half steps, the octave being divided into twelve equal parts. The new tones added between *C* and *D*, *D* and *E*, *F* and *G*, *G* and *A*, and *A* and *B* are called chromatic tones, and are foreign to the key— that is, they are not diatonic tones. Obviously these alien tones are possible only at points where there is an interval of a whole step (a major second). In the major scale there are five such intervals, and therefore five new tones may be added. These, of course, are represented on the staff by sharps, flats, naturals, double sharps, and double flats.

Of the several possible ways of writing this series of tones known as the chromatic scale, the simplest is the notation employed in the melodic form shown below in the keys of *C, D♭* and *E* major.

EX. 14-1

168

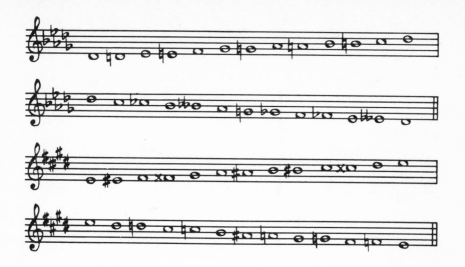

In the ascending scales above, it will be noted that each new chromatic tone is derived from the *lower* diatonic tone immediately preceding, which has been raised. In the descending scale the new tones are derived from the preceding *upper* diatonic tone. The one exception here is that the raised fourth is used instead of the lowered fifth. The names of the chromatic tones are likewise derived from the diatonic tones; for example, *C, C♯, D, D♯,* for the ascending, and *C, B, B♭, A, A♭,* for the descending. To secure the new syllabic names for the raised tones, the original vowels are changed to "i" (pronounced "ee"). For the lowered tones, the vowel is changed to "e" (pronounced "ay"). One exception in this respect is *re,* which already has the vowel "e." When re is lowered, the spelling is changed to *ra* and it is pronounced "rah."

The spelling of the chromatic scale in minor differs from major as shown below in the key of *C* minor:

EX. 14-2

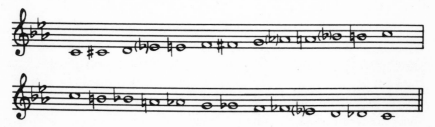

**Augmented and diminished intervals.** In Chapter 11 we learned that an interval from the key tone of the major scale to any other tone of the scale is either major or perfect. The major intervals, we learned, are the second, third, sixth, seventh, and ninth; the perfect intervals, the prime, fourth, fifth, and octave. The minor intervals—the minor second, third, sixth, seventh, and ninth—are the same as the major except that each is a half step smaller than the corresponding major. These are shown below for review.

EX. 14-3

In addition to the three classes of intervals just mentioned, there are two others, the *augmented* and the *diminished*. The augmented intervals have the same general name as the *major* and *perfect,* but are one half step *larger*. The diminished intervals have the same general name as the *minor* and *perfect,* but are one half step *smaller*. These are illustrated below:

EX. 14-4

Intervals may be further classified as consonant and dissonant. The dissonant intervals, because of their active nature, are normally resolved to the consonant. Examining the intervals already discussed on the basis of consonance and dissonance, it may be pointed out that the perfect intervals are called perfect consonants; major and minor thirds and sixths, imperfect consonants; major and minor seconds and sevenths, and all augmented and diminished intervals, dissonances.

[1] These intervals are rare in music because they contain the same number of half steps as a perfect interval. Doubly augmented and diminished intervals also occur in music but quite rarely.

An interval may be inverted by taking the lower tone and placing it an octave higher, or by placing the upper tone an octave lower, as shown in Ex. 14-5 below:

EX. 14-5

It will be noted that when it is inverted the perfect interval remains perfect—hence its name; the major becomes minor; the minor becomes major; the augmented becomes diminished; and the diminished becomes augmented. It should also be noted that the general name is changed in every case: the fifth becomes a fourth, the fourth becomes a fifth, and so on.

## HARMONY

**The mediant chord.** The *mediant chord,* built on the third tone of the scale, is the least important of the secondary triads. It, like the other secondary chords, is minor, having a minor third and a perfect fifth. Its principal use is to harmonize the seventh degree of the scale in a descending passage. It is shown below in fundamental position and first inversion, as it is most frequently found.

EX. 14-6

## RHYTHM

**Review of rhythm.** In the preceding chapters we have studied the typical rhythms as found in the six meters most frequently used in music. These included the various relative note and rest lengths, the divided beat and sub-divided beat, the dotted half, quarter, and eighth, the tie, and the triplet. The melodies found in the accompanying Melodies for Singing illustrate these rhythms and will serve as a review.

# MELODIES FOR SINGING AND DICTATION

The following melodies contain a review of the rhythms studied in previous chapters, chromatic tones, and the chord tones of the mediant triad.

## MELODIES FOR SINGING

Shadow Song   from Dinorah   MEYERBEER

Ah Must Ye Fade   from La Sonnambula   BELLINI

Praise of Tears   SCHUBERT

12 Andante

I Love Thee   GRIEG

13 Andantino

Goodbye   TOSTI

14 Andante con Moto

English Folk Song

15 Andante con Moto
Tenerezza

Songs My Mother Taught Me   DVORAK

# MELODIES FOR DICTATION

# SUGGESTIONS FOR FURTHER STUDY

Write the chromatic scale ascending and descending on the work sheet at (a), in the keys of *F, Eb, Gb, G, D, B* and *F♯* major.

Write the I, II, III, IV, V, V₇ and VI chords in the keys of *Eb,* and *A* major on the work sheet at (b). Indicate the intervals in each chord and show whether it is major or minor. Play the chords, listening to the total effect.

Identify the intervals at (c) on the work sheet.

Invert the intervals at (d) on the work sheet and identify.

Play the chord progressions, Appendix A, No. 12, in all major keys.

Identify the successive intervals in melody No. 4 in Melodies for Singing above.

## WORK SHEET

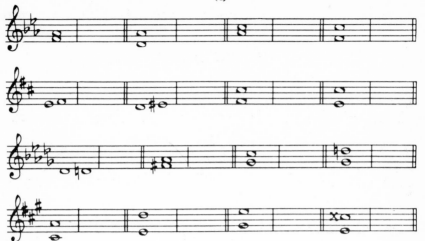

# • 15 •

# Coda

During the preceding fourteen chapters, our study has covered the following fundamentals of music: six meters found most frequently in music; the rhythms common to these meters; tempo; dynamics; the major and minor mode; keys and their signatures; diatonic and chromatic tones; the basic elements of form; the principal and secondary chords; and the various symbols used in the notation of music. These have been introduced as needed for further growth, and they have been illustrated and applied in the melodies for singing and dictation.

The present chapter is somewhat of a summary of what has gone before, but in a new setting—a sort of coda, with a different treatment of material. For example, heretofore we have experienced rhythm only in a simple fashion as it occurs in the melody line; in this chapter we will consider it in a more complex form, as it appears in connection with two or more parts. For example, one part may have two or more notes moving against a single note in another part. In past chapters, also, melody and intervals have been experienced only in unison singing. In this chapter, we will experience them as they are sung in parts. In much the same way, our experience in harmony has been limited to the general or total effect produced as the chords were sounded during the singing of some of the melodies. In this chapter, however, we are to hear these same chords by actually singing them.

It is the sincere hope of the author that the pleasure which the student derives in this chapter from singing familiar rhythms, melodies, and harmonies in new settings will lead him to many more pleasant experiences as he continues the study of music.

**Singing in two parts.** The new settings, or new experiences of what the student has already learned in past chapters, constitute part singing. The first ten melodies that the student will consider are in two parts. In his singing of these melodies he should listen carefully for several effects:

(1) For the intervals as the parts are sung, observing the total effect produced.

(2) For the rhythmic activity of each part as two or more notes in one part are sung against one note in the other.

(3) For repetitions as each part takes his turn in stating, at a higher or lower pitch, what the other has just finished singing. Repetitions are particularly noticeable in melodies 9 and 10. These correspond to exact or sequential repetitions found in melody, but their use here is known as *imitation.* That is, the voices or parts imitate each other.

**Four part melodies.** Four part singing likewise presents a new experience featuring familiar material.

(1) In former chapters the chords were played as the melodies were sung. Now we will hear them as the parts are sung, observing the total effect.

(2) The student should look for the passing and neighboring tones and observe their movement up and down as they move in similar directions. It should also be noted that they move in contrary directions— that is, one part moves up as the other moves down. This is known respectively as *parallel* and *contrary* motion.

(3) In his listening in four part singing, the student should be particularly concerned with the total effect produced by the major and minor chords. He should strive to become conscious of the other parts also being sung.

(4) At the end of each of the first two phrases of melody No. 12, the chord seems hollow or incomplete. The student should try to discover the missing chord tone. If the last chord of this melody comes as a surprise, the student should try to determine why.

(5) The student will note the use of the VII triad in melodies 13 and 14. This chord appears with less frequency than the other triads introduced in this text. It is a diminished chord, its third being minor and its fifth diminished.

# MELODIES FOR SINGING

1  Moderato

*mf*

Easter Hymn  LUTHER-HUSS

2  Moderato

*mf*

Hymn (Lutheran)

182

3   Moderato

Hymn   Lutheran

4   Andante

Chanson du Roi de Navarre   (Unknown)

5  Moderato

*mf*

Luther's Prayer  (Lutheran)

6  Andante

*mp*

184

To the Blessed Trinity   (Unknown)

187

Sweet Nymph Come to Thy Lover MORLEY

9 Andantino

Essex's Last Good-Night  ENGLISH BALLAD

190

V(D)  I(F)  I₆  II(F)  V(F)  I(F)

I(F)  I(F)  I(F)  IV(F) I(F)  I(D)  V(D) I(D)

Daphne  ENGLISH BALLAD

V(D)  I(D)  I(F)  V₆(F)  I(D)  V  I(D)

12 Moderato

mp

I  V  VI  II  I  V  I

Once I loved a Maiden Fair  ENGLISH BALLAD

IV  I₆  I  V  III  VI  II  I  V  I

191

Half Hannikin — English Dance

Stand Thy Ground Old Harry — English Dance

# Appendix A

# Appendix B

# The Fundamentals of Conducting

In addition to the suggestions given in the body of the text regarding the movement of the hand or baton, the beginner should also master the following:

**Fractional part of the beat.** (1) When the music begins on a *fractional part of a beat,* give the preparatory beat, and, with a quick motion of the wrist, indicate when the ensemble is to begin. The breath, as usual, will be taken on the preparatory beat, but will be quicker. It must be remembered that the preparatory beat and any rhythmic cue indications must be in tempo.

**The fermata.** (2) The *fermata* or hold ( ⌒ ) should offer no particular problem. Merely bring the hand to a halt on the beat to be held; release in the direction of this beat, and the hand is in position for the beat which follows. Take as an example:

The fermata occurs on count three; stop the hand there. Just before the release, slightly raise the hand and release in the direction of the third beat. The hand is then in position for the fourth beat. The release actually marks the end of the third beat and rebounds as a beat should. It is this rebound which serves as a preparatory beat on which the ensemble breathes, thus preparing the group to sing or play on the fourth beat.

**The left hand.** (3) The *left hand* should be used to indicate the entrance of various voices or instruments. Such indications should be preceded by the preparatory beat in the left hand so that the performer is made ready. In the case of successive entrances, it is wise to drop the left hand to the side after each entrance. This will make the left hand noticeable when another cue is to be executed.

**Both hands.** (4) In leading community, assembly, or church congregational singing, or in directing large groups, the use of *both hands* may be employed. The hands should be spread apart suggesting an invitation for all the people to participate. The motion of the hands should be *down-up* for duple meter; *down-out-up* for triple; *down-in-out-up* for quadruple. The size of the beat will depend upon the size of the group and the tempo of the music.

**The conductor.** The Conductor is an *interpreter* and a *leader*. This means that he must effectively explain; he must unfold or make clear the meaning of the music and know the techniques of developing through the music an ensemble expression. In doing this he must concern himself with three entities, the *composer,* the *ensemble,* and *himself.* His task is to *discover* and to *develop* to the utmost the beauty and feeling through himself and the performers as originally intended by the composer.

**The composer.** The *composer* is the *first* consideration of the conductor. As interpreter the conductor should:

(1) Determine the *mood* of the music. This results from a combination of the *rhythm, melody, harmony, form, dynamics* and general tone color of the composition.

(2) Ascertain the *style* and *period* through which the composer has expressed himself. When did the composer live, how did he and other composers and artists of his period express themselves?

(3) Fathom the *real meaning* and *emotional levels* contained in the composition. What was the composer really endeavoring to say? His only means of communication was through a group of symbols which at best could only partly convey the real meaning. The conductor must "read between the lines," as it were, in order to ascertain the depth of meaning and feeling expressed in the composition. In this, the conductor's intelligence, imagination, and artistry are put to the test.

(4) *Study* and *analyze* each phrase and each voice part considering their relationship to other parts, determining, in other words, where

the composer has best expressed himself, and where he has placed emphasis.

(5) Examine the *dynamics* to determine the relative loudness and softness of voice parts, phrases, and other divisions of the composition.

**The ensemble.** The *second* consideration for the conductor is the *ensemble* through which he conveys the composer's message. The problems confronting him are:

(1) Does the ensemble have the *background* and *musical ability* to interpret this composition effectively? Is the vocal or instrumental range suitable for this group? Can the ensemble properly execute the rhythm, melody, harmony, and tempo? Can the group fathom the deeper meaning of the music? Will the music challenge the ensemble sufficiently to sustain interest? Does the ensemble have the necessary voices and instruments to emphasize effectively the parts stressed by the composer?

(2) Brief *explanation* of his concept of the composition as a result of his study. When the ensemble is more familiar with the composition, the conductor will ask stimulating questions in an effort to lead each member to understand, feel, and interpret the music.

(3) Develop the *tone quality* or variety of qualities in keeping with the character of the music and/or text. Too often, notes are merely sung or played, regardless of whether the music is bright, gloomy, prayerful, or speaks of love, hope, or hate. Improvement in tone quality is often the result of a thorough understanding of music and text.

(4) Work out *phrasing, breathing,* changes in *tempos,* and *dynamics.*

(5) Concern himself with *balance of parts, pitch, intonation, blend,* correct use of *vowels* and *consonants, attacks,* and *releases.*

Thus, in meeting these requirements the conductor must understand thoroughly both the music and the ensemble, and must unfold to his listeners the hidden beauties of each: the composer's through a sympathetic interpretation of his music, that of the ensemble through a proper attention to its vital, living personality. In the latter respect, he must be skillful in human relationships. Attitude, response, understanding, and co-operation of the participators with him in the composer's music are of great importance.

**Himself.** Yet, although the personality of each individual is important, the stress in this brief discussion must be primarily on the conductor. He is the *third* consideration.

The following outline will serve to suggest three important qualifications of a successful conductor:

(1) *Musicianship.*

    a. Historical and theoretical background of music.

    b. Fundamental principles of vocal and/or instrumental production as applied in the ensemble.

    c. A keen sense of rhythm.

    d. Ability to hear melodic and harmonic intervals.

(2) *Personality.*

    a. A wholesome, cheerful, positive attitude toward life, people, and music.

    b. Ability to see mistakes, including his own, in a humorous light.

    c. Self confidence blended with humility.

    d. Patience, patience, patience!

(3) *General Abilities.*

    a. An understanding of the individual and mass mind.

    b. The ability to inspire others.

    c. A creative imagination.

    d. An ability to organize.

In one sentence: the conductor must be a *musician,* a *psychologist,* and an *organizer,* possessing all of those personal qualities which *pleasantly cause others to do his will.*

As may be easily seen, conducting involves far more than merely "beating time." Yet the conductor must also master—at least—the *conventional conducting patterns* for the various meters. These are the same for both choral and instrumental conducting. By the use of these patterns the conductor informs the ensemble where he is within the measure. Through the character of his beat, eyes, face, and his entire body, he reveals to the group the essential nature of the music. These expressions should be practiced before a mirror by the apprentice conductor until they become a definite part of his personality, wholly expressive of his feelings. Many a beginner endeavors to copy the idiosyncracies of a conductor he admires. But if he is wise, he will find for himself as quickly as possible *his own personality* and thus *freedom* and *control* through these patterns. As with freedom under the law, freedom in this respect begins with control and discipline. He must therefore guard against developing habits which have no meaning, or which in any way attract undue attention to himself and consequently detract from the music.

While leading his group, the conductor should *stand erect* with the weight of the body on the soles of the feet. The over-all posture should be such as to convey *command, security,* and *confidence* to the conductor, performer, and audience. There should be no tention in the wrist, fingers, elbows, or shoulders. The arm should be held slightly away from the ribs and clearly visible to all performers. This position makes for more control and freedom of movement, expansion for breathing, and suggests animation.

Ten conducting precepts:

(1) The time value of tones is determined by the interval of time existing between the beats which extends from the beginning of the one count to the beginning of the next. In the following example, the release of the tied note should be on count two (the rest):

(2) The result of what happens between the beats is either good or bad music and may be indicative of the conductor's hand movements.

(3) The accompanyist should not play while the conductor is giving instructions and should begin only when signaled by him. At this point, the choir and conductor should give full attention, thus showing respect for the music and the accompanyist and gaining the attention of the audience. The attitude should indicate that the composition begins with the accompaniment and is not completed until the release of the final chord. The same attitude and attention should be accorded the soloist.

(4) When the conductor is wrong or makes a mistake, he should admit it. This is a mark of greatness which even small children sense.

(5) The appearance of a group is important from the standpoint of the audience as well as the group. A neat, clean appearance in attractive uniform dress may actually improve tone quality.

(6) Talk less; sing and play more.

(7) Make corrections in all sincerity; compliment and express appreciation to the ensemble.

(8) Sarcasm marks a conductor as "little" and comes back to him in a cynical group attitude and in a poor tone quality.

(9) The conductor should keep his eyes upon the group; and the ensemble should keep their eyes upon him.

(10) The conductor and the ensemble should thoroughly enjoy the activity if desirable vitality and an effect of spontaneity is created through the performance.

# Index